Eight Women of Faith

Eight Women
of Faith

Michael A. G. Haykin

WHEATON, ILLINOIS

Cover design: Connie Gabbert

First printing 2016

Printed in the United States of America

Trade paperback ISBN: 978-1-4335-4892-5
epub ISBN: 978-1-4335-4895-6
PDF ISBN: 978-1-4335-4893-2
Mobipocket ISBN: 978-1-4335-4894-9

Library of Congress Cataloging-in-Publication Data
Names: Haykin, Michael A. G., author.
Title: Eight women of faith / Michael A.G. Haykin.
Description: Wheaton : Crossway, 2016. | Includes bibliographical references and index.
Identifiers: LCCN 2016000448 (print) | LCCN 2016012254 (ebook) | ISBN 9781433548925 (tp) |
    ISBN 9781433548956 (ePub) | ISBN 9781433548932 (pdf) | ISBN 9781433548949 (mobi)
Subjects: LCSH: Christian women—Biography. | Women in Christianity.
Classification: LCC BR1713 .H39 2016 (print) | LCC BR1713 (ebook) | DDC 270.092/52—dc23
LC record available at http://lccn.loc.gov/2016000448

Crossway is a publishing ministry of Good News Publishers.

VP		26	25	24	23	22	21	20	19	18	17	16
15	14	13	12	11	10	9	8	7	6	5	4	3	2

So God created man in his own image,
in the image of God created he him;
male and female created he them.

Genesis 1:27 (KJV)

To John Friesen, Bev Offner, and
the staff and guests of Muskoka Bible Centre,
Huntsville, Ontario
2008–2015

Contents

Foreword

Genesis 2 tells us that God created a garden with "every tree that is pleasant to the sight and good for food" (v. 9). God told Adam to eat freely of every tree except one. But rather than focusing on the abundance God had offered freely, Adam and Eve turned their focus on the single thing that was off-limits. And the rest is human history.

Both within the church and outside it, we too have treated in a similar fashion the biblical admonition against women preaching: we focus on the single thing that is off-limits and thereby fail to see the abundant opportunities and roles God *has* clearly offered, some of which are compellingly portrayed in the stories presented in this book. Likewise, the biblical admonition has led too often to extrabiblical limitations on women, as well as unbiblical oppression, also reflected in the societal restraints these eight women experienced during their lives. This kind of failure toward women—unjustly imposed limitations on their personhood and soul equality—has sometimes led to a secondary failure: the failure to see and tell women's stories clearly, truthfully, and well.

Thus, there exists an abundance of works on the lives of women in the church that present readers with unrealistic saints, not flesh-and-blood women. Such accounts make good fairy tales but not just or suitable examples of the true life of faith. On the other hand, much of today's retrospectives on women in history tend to focus, understandably and sometimes rightly, on limitations placed on women. Women have been and still are denied much, both in the church and in the culture at large.

This book's snapshots of a mere eight women from a mere two centuries offer an astonishing array of roles and achievements by women in a time when women were not so much second-class citizens as not citizens at all. Yet despite (and perhaps because of) such obstacles, what women have contributed and accomplished is rich and varied. Here in these pages we meet queen, wife, theologian, hymnist, novelist, missionary, daughter, and friend. Even more importantly, we meet women of faith whose lives manifested the grace and glory of God through their faithful obedience to the roles to which they were called, whether in singleness or marriage, in sickness or in health, in riches or in poverty, and, ultimately, in death.

The facets of womanhood represented in *Eight Women of Faith* shine brilliantly. This abundance is particularly striking within the early modern era represented by the lives detailed here. The period hinges on a significant turning point in both human history and church history: the Protestant Reformation. The Reformation's emphasis on faith alone and Scripture alone gave birth to the modern individual (and thus the evangelical tradition)—and it is the lives of women that most clearly reflect the dramatic historical shifts that took place as a result. It is women of faith, particularly evangelical faith (with its emphasis on individual salvation), who mirror most clearly this great shift in human history and culture that elevated human agency and equality. These developments drew me to my own study on an evangelical woman of this era, Hannah More, the British poet, abolitionist, and reformer of the late eighteenth and early nineteenth centuries—and they drew me to this fascinating work as well.

The portraits Haykin paints of these wildly different women reduce them neither to their roles nor to their religion, but rather show how their faith informed, shaped, and fulfilled their earthly callings. Furthermore, regardless of their relationships to men (single, married, wife, daughter, mother), the women are presented as individuals in their own right, as influenced as they are influential in the roles they fill. Margaret Baxter and Sarah Edwards, for example, are shown as faithful servants of the gospel who are as much served by as servants to their respective husbands, Richard Baxter and Jonathan Edwards. The theology embodied by the written works of Anne Dutton, Anne Steele, and Jane Austen models the abundance in God's garden: we can obey the command not to eat the forbidden fruit and still enjoy a feast abundant enough to nourish all of the faithful.

The lives here demonstrate the truth of Jane Austen's words, applicable to men and women equally, that "Christians should be up and doing something in the world." The women in this book, each in her own way, did just that. After reading about them, you will want to, too.

Karen Swallow Prior
Liberty University, Virginia

Introduction

The word *feminism* first appeared in the English language in the late nineteenth century.[1] Yet debates about the role and status of women in society had been going on for a considerable period of time before that. Take, for example, the historical era of the British Civil Wars (1638–1651) and the Republican government of the Puritan Oliver Cromwell (1599–1658) that followed these wars in the 1650s. It is a period of history that has been well described as "a world turned upside down." Questions were raised about so much that had been taken for granted, and among these questions were ones about the role of women.

The Quakers and Women Preachers

The Quakers, for example, who emerged as a potent force in the 1650s, proclaimed that there were no spiritual differences between men and women, and therefore there should be no distinction in ministry. Margaret Fell (1614–1702), wife of the Quaker leader George Fox (1624–1691), asserted her right to preach in her best-known work *Women's Speaking Justified, Proved and Allowed of by the Scriptures* (London, 1666),[2] as did a few other Quaker women in the 1640s and 1650s, like Elizabeth Fletcher (c. 1638–1658) in Oxford and Martha Simmonds in London, and this sometimes against Quaker male leadership.[3] Jacqueline Broad has noted that Margaret Fell's arguments in favour of female preaching rest on a principle of spiritual equality, or the idea that both men and women have the supernatural light of Christ within them. But for Fell, the ability to hearken to that light implicitly requires that women possess a natural capacity to discern the truth for themselves, to exercise strength of will, and to exhibit moral virtue or excellence of character. In these respects, Fell's arguments for female preaching contain an implicit feminist challenge to negative perceptions about women's moral and intellectual abilities in her time.[4]

Puritan Response to Quaker Views about Women Preachers

This brief discussion of the Quakers is significant, for Quaker women preachers reinforced in the mind of more mainstream Puritans, like the Baptists, that having female preachers was definitely wrong.[5] In 1645, before the emergence of the Quakers, when representatives of the Calvinistic Baptist churches in what is known as the Western Association met, the question was asked whether a woman could speak in the church. The reply was clear: "A woman is not permitted to speak at all in the church, neither by way of praying, prophesying, enquiring, 1 Cor. 14.34f., 1 Tim. 2.11f."[6] The same question was raised ten or so years later, after the Quaker movement had begun. This time it was the Midland Association where the question was asked. The same answer was basically given along with the reason for women's silence: the "inferiority of their sex" and to prevent any "usurping of authority over men." Nevertheless, five exceptions were given when a woman could speak in church:

1. To publicly give a testimony of conversion when seeking baptism and church membership.
2. To give a report if she had been involved in seeking the restoration of a wayward church member.
3. If she had been sent with a message from another congregation (are they thinking of Phoebe here, Romans 16:1–2?)
4. If she needed the church's help and had to lay out that need before the church.

5. If she had been "disfellowshiped" because of sin and was seeking forgiveness by the congregation and reconciliation.[7]

Women Essential to Puritan Nonconformity

Despite these restrictions, in mainstream Puritan groups—Baptists, as well as Congregationalists and Presbyterians—women did play critical roles in two key areas. First, they played a critical role in teaching children and servants in the home in accord with the marginal note in the Geneva Bible's rendering of Deuteronomy 21:18, "It is the mother's duty also to instruct her children."[8] Proponents of the state church feared this Puritan emphasis on the family as a school of piety, for, in their minds, it weakened the parish church.[9]

Then, in opening their homes to Puritan ministers, women often played a key role in the establishment of Puritan congregations. For example, Mrs. Dorothy Hazzard (d. 1675) seceded from the parish church of her husband, Matthew Hazzard, in 1640 to establish what later became Broadmead Baptist Church. The church actually began with Hazzard and four men meeting in the Hazzard home, which, of course, was also the home of the parish minister! Within three years the church had 160 members. Not surprisingly, this congregation also appointed deaconesses in the 1660s and 1670s. The first deaconess to be appointed was Mary West in 1662. After her death she was replaced in 1673 by a "Sister Murry," and by 1679 three more women had been appointed. Following 1 Timothy 5:9, these women were required to be widows over the age of sixty who agreed not to pursue remarriage. They were to take care of the physical needs of the sick in the congregation and be ready to "speak a word to their souls as occasion requires."[10] As Patricia Crawford rightly concludes, "women were essential to Nonconformity," both its emergence and its growth.[11]

The Apostle Paul and the Modern Day

The key roles that women played in the advance of Puritan and Nonconformist congregations have strong biblical precedent. For instance, a close reading of Romans 16:1–16 reveals the truth of the remark by Roger Gryson that "there is no doubt that Paul was the beneficiary of numerous instances of assistance from women in his work as an apostle."[12] Of the twenty-seven believers mentioned here in Romans 16, ten of them are women, with a number of them being commended for their hard work in the Lord (Mary, v. 6; Tryphaena and Tryphosa, v. 12a; Persis, v. 12b) and others being especially recognized for their help to Paul (Phoebe, vv. 1–2; Priscilla, vv. 3–4; Rufus's mother, v. 13b). Paul's remarks in this chapter of Romans have to be viewed against the cultural milieu of his day that frequently disparaged women.

Today, thankfully, the misogynistic trends of certain areas of Western culture have been challenged, and the issues that Christians face in this regard are somewhat different from those of Paul. A strong feminist movement in Western culture has effectively produced a crisis of masculinity in many areas of Western thinking. From the disparagement of women, our culture has swung in many respects to the opposite extreme, the disparagement of men. And in the midst of this, the church needs to be found faithful to the biblical witness. In a culture being swamped by a tsunami of feminism, the great danger for the church is to have a knee-jerk reaction and fail to appreciate what the apostolic generation, and our Puritan and Nonconformist forebears knew: the vital importance of women for the life of the church.

The Genesis and Nature of This Book

This book—really an extended essay comprising eight different historical and textual vignettes—seeks to remind contemporary Christians, especially evangelicals, of the vital role that women have played in the history of our faith. Although I began lecturing in the 1990s on women in church history, the immediate inspiration for this book lies in a suggestion made to me by my good friend Jim Fraser, a high school teacher on the Simcoe County School Board, during a week that I was teaching at Muskoka Bible Centre, Ontario, in the summer of 2013. He pointed out that Eric Metaxas had just brought out his *Seven Men: And the Secret of Their Greatness*,[13] and that I should do a comparable book on women. I was eager to follow up on this suggestion as I recognized the real need for such a book in the life of the church. I am very thankful for Jim's ongoing encouragement of my writing on this topic.

I had come across past books such as Samuel Burder's *Memoirs of Eminently Pious Women of the British Empire* (1823), a three-volume expansion of an earlier volume by Thomas Gibbons that had first been published in 1777. But books like this were long out of print. Much more recently Jamie Janosz wrote *When Others Shuddered: Eight Women Who Refused to Give Up*,[14] which focuses on eight nineteenth-century figures. In many ways I felt that earlier centuries, especially the eighteenth century, were critical to investigate, especially due to the fact that it was in the eighteenth century that Western culture launched into the "brave new" project of reconfiguring society entirely on the basis of human reason and experience. How did Christian women in that era respond to the challenges around them?

The book that you hold in your hands is the result of the interplay of these past events and suggestions. Along the way I have been privileged to teach some of this material not only in my classes at Southern Baptist Theological Seminary but also in one-day conferences at Calvary Baptist Church of Lenexa, Kansas (thanks to Pastor Brian Albert especially), and Emmanuel Baptist Church, Otisville, Michigan (thanks to Pastor Leroy Cole). A good portion of these chapters was also given in morning sessions of a Bible week at the Muskoka Bible Centre in the summer of 2014, and I am deeply thankful to John Friesen, CEO of the Centre, for the opportunity to do this and for all of the MBC staff who helped facilitate this. Finally, I am very thankful also to Linda Reed for the invitation to coteach a course, "The Great Women of the Christian Faith," this past June at Heritage Theological Seminary, which helped me to focus the chapters of this book.

In some ways, the book falls into two parts. The first two chapters, those on Lady Jane Grey and Margaret Charlton Baxter, explore women's lives in the church prior to the significant changes of the eighteenth century. Jane speaks of the way that women made the faith of the Reformation their own, and Margaret shows how women helped men in ministry, in this case, her husband, Richard Baxter. I explore these themes by looking at certain written texts, either by the two women or about them. The next six chapters then constitute a prolonged essay on what it was like to be a Christian woman in the eighteenth century, and written texts again play a central role in the chapters. Anne Dutton, a highly competent theological author, helped serve as a spiritual guide through her books; Sarah Edwards, who left virtually no print footstep, nonetheless reveals the way some Christian women have had profound experiences of God for the blessing of the church; Anne Steele is a pioneer of women hymn writers, in which women helped the church worship through song and melody; the diary of Esther Edwards Burr, the daughter of Sarah Edwards, is a fabulous window on the vista of Christian friendship, a long-neglected area of Christian living. Ann Judson was a pioneer missionary with her husband and became something of an icon for generations of women missionaries who followed her; and, finally, there is a chapter on Jane Austen, far and away the most famous of all of the women in this book, who was also a serious Christian, though this is not often remembered.

May the Holy Spirit be pleased to use this book for the good of both men and women in the church of the Lord Jesus.

Dundas, Ontario
July 31, 2015

1

The Witness of Jane Grey, an Evangelical Queen

"Faith Only Justifieth"

It is February 10 in the year 1554. We are in a room in the Tower of London, where the Lady Jane Grey (1537–1554), who had been Queen of England for little over a week the previous year—from July 10–19, 1553—is imprisoned. She has been condemned to death by her cousin Mary I (1516–1558), also known to history as "Bloody Mary." Though Mary, a die-hard Roman Catholic, is determined to end Jane's earthly life, Mary also wants to save Jane's soul. So she has sent one of her most able chaplains, a Benedictine monk by the name of John Feckenham (c. 1515–1584), to speak to Jane and convince her of her theological errors.[1] Feckenham was no stranger to theological debate, since he had debated a number of leading Protestant theologians in the early 1550s, men such as John Hooper (1500–1555) and John Jewel (1522–1571). He may well have thought that a young woman such as Jane would be hard-pressed to withstand the power of his reasoning.

Jane recorded the conversation after Feckenham left her. According to Jane's account—and we do not have a similar account from Feckenham, though there seems no reason to doubt the veracity of Jane's recollection—after Jane had confessed her faith in the triunity of God, she affirmed that people are saved by faith alone. Feckenham responded to this by citing 1 Corinthians 13:2, "If I have all faith . . . but have not love, I am nothing." In other words, Feckenham was maintaining that salvation was the result of both faith and love shown by good works. Jane stood her ground:

> Jane: True it is, for how can I love him in whom I trust not? Or how can I trust in him whom I love not? Faith and love agreeth both together, and yet love is comprehended in faith.
>
> Feckenham: How shall we love our neighbour?
>
> Jane: To love our neighbour is to feed the hungry, clothe the naked, and give drink to the thirsty, and to do to him as we would do to ourselves.
>
> Feckenham: Why then it is necessary to salvation to do good works and it is not sufficient to believe.
>
> Jane: I deny that and I affirm that faith only saves. But it is meet for Christians, in token that they follow their master Christ, to do good works, yet may we not say that they profit to salvation. For, although we have all done all that we can, yet we be unprofitable servants, and the faith only in Christ's blood saveth.[2]

Who was this remarkable young woman and how did she come to be in this precarious position in the infamous Tower of London? In some ways, Jane's story is a difficult one to tell since it cannot be understood without due consideration of the politics swirling her life. So as we remember her story, while our focus is going to be on her Christian faith, the political scene cannot be ignored. Jane was the granddaughter of Henry VIII's (1491–1547) youngest and favorite sister, Mary Tudor (1496–1533), and was thus that wily monarch's great-niece. During Jane's life she stood fourth in line to the English throne after Henry's three children— Edward VI (1537–1553), Mary, and Elizabeth (1533–1603)—and was elevated to the crown after the death of her cousin Edward VI in 1553. Thus any consideration of Jane's life inevitably involves looking at the politics of the day.

Jane's Early Days

Jane Grey was born to Henry Grey (1517–1554), the Marquis of Dorset, and his wife, Frances (1517–1559), the niece of Henry VIII, at their palatial Leicestershire home, Bradgate Manor, early in October 1537. She appears to have been named after the queen of the day, Jane Seymour (c. 1508–1537), the third wife of Henry VIII and the mother of the future Edward VI.

Jane's parents were highly ambitious, callous individuals who balked at nothing to get ahead. They initially hoped that they could marry Jane off to Henry VIII's only son, Edward, who had been born in the same month as Jane. Thus Jane's parents imposed on her a rigid system of education, requiring her to master Latin, Greek, French, and Italian, so as to make her attractive to the future monarch. In 1546, when Jane was nine, she was sent to Henry's court to live under the guardianship of Queen Katharine Parr (1512–1548), the sixth and final wife of Henry VIII. All of this was part of her parents' selfish scheme to marry her to Edward and so advance their standing in society. But in the providence of God this led to Jane's coming under the influence of Katharine Parr, one of the most charming and intelligent women of the day, a woman who, moreover, was a genuine Christian. In the words of one of her chaplains: "Her rare goodness has made every day a Sunday."[3] It appears to have been the case that it was during this stay in the household of Queen Katharine that Jane came to a living faith in Christ.[4] As Paul Zahl has noted, Katherine was "Jane's real mother in Christianity."[5]

In 1547, though, Katherine Parr was widowed as Henry VIII died, and as a result Jane soon returned to her parents' home. Henry was succeeded by his son Edward, who was crowned Edward VI on February 20, 1547. He was but nine years of age. Yet he was surrounded by a number of godly counselors, including Thomas Cranmer (1489–1556), the Archbishop of Canterbury, who was determined to make England a bastion of the Reformed faith.[6] The great French Reformer John Calvin (1509–1564) actually wrote a letter to Edward's guardian, his uncle Edward Seymour (c. 1500–1552), in which he likened Edward VI to King Josiah. And in time the young English monarch was indeed like Josiah, eager to have his subjects learn biblical truth. Of a hundred or so extant treatises from Edward's hand, a number clearly evidence Edward's commitment to the evangelical faith.

When Jane returned to her parents' home in Bradgate, they seem to have considered her a "symbol of failure and a wasted effort—and they treated her accordingly."[7] Jane's response was to pour herself into her studies. She began to excel in Greek and even entered into correspondence with such continental Reformers as Martin Bucer (1491–1551), then living in Cambridge, and Heinrich Bullinger (1504–1575) of Zurich.[8] She was growing in grace and becoming articulate in her faith, though there is also evidence that she was strong-minded and at times displayed a very stubborn streak like many of her Tudor relatives.[9]

Marriage and Edward's Death

In the spring of 1552, King Edward had the measles, and, not taking time to recover, he soon began to show symptoms of tuberculosis. As the year wore on, it became increasingly clear to those who were close to the king that he would not reach adulthood. Now, Henry VIII's will had named his daughter Mary as next in line to the throne. If Edward did not marry and produce an heir, a Catholic would rule England. Edward's Chief Minister, John Dudley (1504–1553), the Duke of Northumberland, well knew that he would be punished by Mary for his support of the Protestant cause. He began to seek a way to prevent her being queen. Jane Grey was fourth in line to the throne and represented, for Northumberland, his only real chance to retain the power and status he had attained. He thus began to foster a close association with Henry and Frances Grey and in due time convinced them to wed their daughter Jane to his son, Guildford Dudley (1535–1554).

Early in May 1553, Jane was told by her parents that she was to be married to Guildford. Though Jane protested and utterly refused, for she despised Guildford, it was ultimately to no avail. After her father had sworn at her and cursed her, and her mother had given her an awful beating, she relented.[10] So it was that on May 25, 1553, Jane was married to Guildford at Durham House in London.

Eight weeks later, on Thursday, July 6, 1553, the fifteen-year-old King Edward died, surrounded by his counselors, who had gathered at his bedside. In his final days, encouraged by John Dudley, but also very much in accord with his own thinking, he had changed his father's will and made Jane his heir. Both of his half-sisters, Mary and Elizabeth, had been disinherited by their father before Henry VIII's death, and Thomas Cranmer, the Archbishop of Canterbury, had declared both of them illegitimate, and thus technically neither could inherit the throne.[11]

News of Edward's death was kept from Jane until Sunday, July 9, when she was informed that she had to go to the Duke of Northumberland's residence, Syon House at Isleworth on the Thames. When, two hours later, Jane entered Syon House from the riverside, she first went into what was known as the Great Hall. Gradually the room filled with people familiar to Jane, including members of the Privy Council and her immediate family, who all pledged to defend with their very lives her right to the throne

Overwhelmed with the news of the death of her cousin, the king, and coupled with the shock of hearing herself proclaimed queen, Jane fainted. None apparently went to help her until she eventually revived by herself and stood up and adamantly maintained that she was not the rightful queen. That was Mary's right. Dudley responded: "Your Grace doth wrong to yourself and to your house." He then recounted the terms of Edward's will, which named her as his heir. Jane's parents joined in, demanding that she accept. At this, she knelt in prayer and found the inner strength to say a little while later, while still kneeling: "If what hath been given me is lawfully mine, may thy divine Majesty grant me such grace that I may govern to thy glory and service, to the advantage of this realm."[12]

Queen Jane

The following day Jane was rowed up the Thames to the Tower of London, where monarchs traditionally stayed until their coronation day. Proclamation was made to the people of London that "Jane, by the grace of God, [is] Queen of England, France and Ireland, Defender of the Faith and of the Church of England and Ireland, under Christ on Earth, the Supreme Head." Most of them would have been quite surprised since Jane was hardly known in the capital. Moreover, they would have regarded Mary as the rightful heir despite the fact that she had been disinherited.

From Sunday, July 9, to Wednesday, July 19, Lady Jane Grey was queen. She signed a few documents, perhaps six in all; she dined once in state and made one or two appointments. She also resolutely refused to agree to the request of her husband and the violent demand of her mother-in-law that Guildford Dudley should be made king.

As soon as Mary had heard of Jane being made queen, however, she marched on London with an army, and all but one or two of those courtiers who had sworn to defend her to the death melted away in the face of Mary's military might. Even Jane's own father declared Mary the rightful queen, hoping that he could escape with his life.[13] It is noteworthy that Thomas Cranmer, the Archbishop of Canterbury, did not desert Jane to her foes. As for Jane herself, an eyewitness account indicates that she seemed relieved that she was no longer queen. Naïvely, she hoped she could simply return to her home. But Mary—soon to be Mary I—did not trust her and committed her to prison in the tower.

Jane Condemned to Death

On July 24, Jane's father-in-law, Dudley, who had been arrested, was also brought to the tower as a prisoner. In the hope of securing a pardon from the queen he recanted his Protestant beliefs, saying that he had been seduced "by the false and erroneous teachings" of the evangelicals. He requested the right to attend mass, which was granted by Mary. With disgust, Jane watched from her window in the tower as he was escorted to mass, and she was heard to say, "I pray God I, nor no friend of mine die so." Dudley was granted a small reprieve, but he could not escape death. He was beheaded on August 23, 1553.

Jane and her husband, Guildford, Dudley's son, were put on trial on November 13. Both were found guilty and sentenced to death. But Jane really did not expect to die in such a way, and initially Mary probably had little intention of carrying out the sentence. But a civil uprising known as the Wyatt Rebellion changed her mind. Sir Thomas Wyatt (1521–1554) raised a small band of soldiers in Kent who were angered when they heard Mary was planning to marry King Philip II (1527–1598) of Spain. In their minds, to have a Spanish Catholic King on the English throne was utterly unthinkable.

Wyatt was able to win his way to London by February 7, 1554. But when he entered the capital, townspeople of London refused to countenance his cause, and the rebellion collapsed. Now, intimately involved in this rebellion was Jane's father, Henry Grey. His involvement all but determined Mary to take Jane's life. On February 7, 1554, Mary accordingly signed the death warrants of "Guilford Dudley and his wife." When Henry Grey was executed, it should be noted, he affirmed that he died "in the faith of Christ, trusting to be saved by his blood only (and not by any trumpery)."[14]

The Conversation with Feckenham

It was thus that Jane met John Feckenham a few days later, after her death warrant had been signed, and had the conversation noted earlier. The full conversation runs as follows:

> Feckenham first speaketh: What thing is required in a Christian?
>
> Jane: To believe in God the Father, in God the Son, in God the Holy Ghost, three persons and one God.
>
> Feckenham: Is there nothing else required in a Christian, but to believe in God?
>
> Jane: Yes, we must believe in him, we must love him with all our heart, with all our soul and all our mind, and our neighbor as ourself.
>
> Feckenham: Why then faith justifieth not, nor saveth not.
>
> Jane: Yes, verily, faith (as St. Paul saith) only justifieth.
>
> Feckenham: Why St. Paul saith: If I have all faith without love, it is nothing.
>
> Jane: True it is, for how can I love him in whom I trust not? Or how can I trust in him whom I love not? Faith and love agreeth both together, and yet love is comprehended in faith.
>
> Feckenham: How shall we love our neighbour?
>
> Jane: To love our neighbour is to feed the hungry, clothe the naked, and give drink to the thirsty, and to do to him as we would do to ourselves.
>
> Feckenham: Why then it is necessary to salvation to do good works and it is not sufficient to believe.

Jane: I deny that and I affirm that faith only saveth. But it is meet for Christians, in token that they follow their master Christ, to do good works, yet may we not say that they profit to salvation. For although we have all done all that we can, yet we be unprofitable servants, and the faith only in Christ's blood saveth.

Feckenham: How many sacraments be there?

Jane: Two, the one the sacrament of baptism, and the other the sacrament of our Lord's supper.

Feckenham: No, there be seven.[15]

Jane: By what Scripture find you that?

Feckenham: Well, we will talk thereof hereafter. But what is signified by your two sacraments?

Jane: By the sacrament of baptism, I am washed with water and regenerated by the Sprit, and that washing is a token to me, that I am the child of God. The sacrament of the Lord's supper is offered unto me as a sure seal and testimony, that I am by the blood of Christ, which he shed for me on the cross, made partaker of the everlasting kingdom.

Feckenham: Why, what do you receive in that bread? Do you not receive the very body and blood of Christ?

Jane: No surely, I do not believe so. I think that at that supper I receive neither flesh, nor blood, but only bread and wine. The which bread when it is broken, and the wine when it is drunk, putteth me in mind, how that for my sins the body of Christ was broken, and his blood shed on the cross, and, with that bread and wine, I receive the benefits that came by [the] breaking of his body, and the shedding of his blood on the cross for my sins.

Feckenham: Why, doth not Christ speak these words: "Take, eat, this is my body?"[16] Require we any plainer words? Doth not he say that it is his body?

Jane: I grant he saith so, and so he saith: "I am the vine, I am the door,"[17] but yet he is never the more the vine nor door. Doth not St. Paul say that he calleth those things that are not as though they were?[18] God forbid that I should say that I eat the very natural body and blood of Christ, for then either I should pluck away my redemption, either else there were two bodies, or two Christs or else two bodies, the one body was tormented on the cross, and then, if they did eat another body, then either he had two bodies, either else if his body were eaten, it was not broken upon the cross, or else if it were broken upon the cross, it was not eaten of his disciples.

Feckenham: Why is it not as possible that Christ by his power could make his body both to be eaten and broken, as to be born of a woman without the seed of man, and as to walk on the sea, having a body, and other such like miracles as he wrought by his power only?

Jane: Yes, verily, if God would have done at his supper a miracle, he might have done so, but I say he minded no work or miracle but only to break his body and shed his blood on the cross for our sins. But I pray you answer me to this one question, Where was Christ when he said: "Take, eat, this is my body"? Was he not at the table when he said so? He was at that time alive, and suffered not till the next day. Well, what took he, but bread? And what break he, but bread? And what gave he, but bread? Look what he took, he break, and look what he break, he gave; and look what he gave, that did they eat; and yet all this while he himself was at supper before his disciples, or else they were deceived.

Feckenham: You ground your faith upon such authors as say and unsay, both with a breath, and not upon the church, to whom you ought to give credit.

Jane: No. I ground my faith upon God's Word and not upon the church. For if the church be a good church, the faith of the church must be tried by God's Word, and not God's Word by the church, neither yet my faith. Shall I believe the church because of antiquity? Or shall I give credit to that church that taketh away from me that half part of the Lord's supper, and will let no laymen receive it in both kinds but themselves? Which thing if they deny to us, they deny us part of our salvation, and I say that is an evil church, and not the spouse of Christ, but the spouse of the devil, that altereth the Lord's supper, and both taketh from it and addeth to it. To that church I say God will add plagues, and from that church will he take their part out of the Book of Life. Do you not learn that of St. Paul, when he ministered it to the Corinthians in both kinds?[19] Shall I believe that church? God forbid.

Feckenham: That was done of a good intent of the church to avoid an heresy that sprung on it.

Jane: Why, shall the church alter God's will and ordinances for a good intent? How did King Saul the Lord define?

With these and such like persuasions, he would have had me to have leaned to the church, but it would not be. There were many mo[re] things whereof we reasoned, but these were the chief.[20]

This conversation is important, for it shows the way that Jane had clearly embraced the key doctrines of the Reformation as her own. According to Paul Zahl, there may well have been a number of others present at this conversation, and thus it might have been akin to the public debates that took place between Roman Catholics and Protestants during the Reformation era.[21] This would explain the way the conversation highlights three key areas of dispute during the Reformation: How are men and women saved? What is the meaning of the Lord's Supper? And upon what basis does one affirm answers to these questions?

As to how a person is saved, Jane maintains what had become

the standard evangelical perspective: people are saved by faith alone. It is not faith and love or faith and good works that save, but faith alone. This faith involves both love and good works, in that true faith issues in works of love and goodness. But Jane affirms unequivocally that salvation is first and foremost based on simple trust in God.

Then in the second area of debate between Jane and Feckenham, Jane maintains that the Lord's Supper is a memorial—"[It] putteth me in mind"—and a vehicle of assurance—it is "a sure seal and testimony," and not at all an event where Christ's physical body and blood become present to the believer. This was a decisive issue of the Reformation: What is the nature of the Lord's Supper, and how is Christ present at his Table?[22] Though they could not agree among themselves as to the nature of Christ's presence, all of the Reformers denied the late medieval Roman Catholic doctrine of transubstantiation, that the bread and wine became the very body and blood of Christ during the course of the celebration of the Lord's Table. Jane also by implication denied this doctrine when she rejected the idea of the ubiquity of Christ's body.[23]

The Reformers also opposed the Roman Catholic practice of offering only the bread and not the wine to the laity during the Lord's Supper, a practice that had become almost uniform by the late Middle Ages. For Jane, Roman Catholic practice in this regard was an indication that the Church of Rome was the spouse of the Devil, not of Christ, since she flagrantly altered Christ's commands. This is part of a larger discussion that Feckenham had introduced by saying that Jane was listening, not to the church, but to various individual authors, whom he would have regarded as heretics. The question at the heart of the exchange between Jane and Feckenham at this point had to do with the source of authoritative doctrine. For Feckenham, that source was indeed Holy Scripture, but Scripture as it was interpreted by authorized teachers of the church. Jane, on the other hand, insisted that she was basing her views on the Word of God alone. And it was by this Word that all doctrine had to be tested. She clearly rejected the view that only those doctrines were to be believed that were approved by the Roman Catholic Church.

Before Feckenham left, he told her he was sorry for her, since, he said, "I am sure we two shall meet," that is, meet in heaven, as he regarded Jane as a heretic. In the face of death, though, Jane's faith shone out clearly, and she replied:

> Truth it is that we shall never meet, unless God turn your heart. For I am sure (unless you repent and turn to God), you are in an evil case, and I pray God, in the bowels of his mercy, to send you his Holy Spirit. For he hath given you his great gift of utterance, if it please him to open the eyes of your heart to his truth.[24]

Feckenham was so impressed by Jane's courage that he asked if he could escort her to the scaffold on the day of her execution, which was to be February 12. Jane agreed, for Mary had refused her request to have an evangelical minister accompany her.[25]

Some Final Words

That night Jane wrote in her Greek New Testament a letter for her younger sister Katherine (1540–1568):

> I have here sent you, good sister Katherine, a book, which although it be not outwardly trimmed with gold, yet inwardly it is more worth than precious stones. It is the book, dear sister, of the Law of the Lord. It is his testament and last will, which he bequeathed unto us wretches, which shall lead you to the path of eternal joy. And if you with a good mind read it, and with an earnest desire follow it, it shall bring you to an immortal and everlasting life. It will teach you to live and learn you to die.
>
> . . . And as touching my death, rejoice as I do, good sister, that I shall be delivered of this corruption, and put on

incorruption. For I am assured that I shall for losing of a mortal life, win an immortal life.[26]

Here we see three things about Jane's faith. She shared the Reformation love of the Scriptures: "It is more worth than precious stones." Then central to this love was Jane's clear understanding as to why the Bible was given to humanity by God: to lead sinners—those whom Jane called "us wretches"—to "eternal joy" and "immortal and everlasting life." And then we also see here Jane's deep assurance of salvation, which the Reformers also generally affirmed.

Why did Jane have such assurance? Well, a final document she wrote on the eve of her execution tells us. She wrote the following three sentences in her prayer book, the first in Latin, the second in Greek, and the final one in English:

> If justice is done with my body, my soul will find mercy with God. Death will give pain to my body for its sins, but the soul will be justified before God. If my faults deserve punishment, my youth at least, and my imprudence, were worthy of excuse; God and posterity will show me favour.[27]

She had assurance of salvation because she was justified before God, that is, made right with God, and was therefore confident of his favor.

Jane's Earthly End

Shortly before eleven o'clock on the morning of February 12, Sir John Brydges (1492–1557), the Lieutenant of the Tower of London, came to lead Jane out to the scaffold that had been built against the wall of the central White Tower, at its northwest corner (the corner closest to the Chapel of St Peter-ad-Vincula).[28] At the scaffold, Jane was met by Feckenham, along with several other Roman Catholic chaplains. An observer recorded what then took place.

She mounted the scaffold stairs and standing there in that chill February morning, Jane briefly addressed the small crowd gathered and urged them to know that she died "a true Christian woman" and that "I do look to be saved by no other mean, but only by the mercy of God, in the blood of his only Son Jesus Christ." She then knelt and recited the fifty-first psalm in English. Feckenham followed in Latin, after which she told him, "God I beseech Him abundantly reward you for your kindness to me." Feckenham was at a complete loss for words and began to weep. Seeing his distress, Jane apparently leaned over and kissed him on the cheek, and for a few moments the Roman Catholic chaplain and the evangelical queen stood hand in hand.[29] She then gave her gloves to a lady-in-waiting and her prayer book to Sir John Brydges. The executioner, after he had asked Jane for forgiveness, which she gave, told Jane to stand near the execution block. She knelt, fumbling to tie a handkerchief around her eyes. Once blindfolded she should have been directly in front of the execution block and could have easily laid her neck in the groove on the block. But she had misjudged the distance. Unable to locate the block, she became anxious. "Where is it? What shall I do? Where is it?" she asked, her voice faltering. No one moved to help her—perhaps unwilling to be an abettor in her death.[30] Finally, after what must have seemed an eternity, a bystander leaped onto the scaffold and guided her to the block. Her last words were called out in a clear voice, "Lord, into thy hands I commend my spirit."

2

Richard Baxter's Testimony about Margaret Baxter[1]

"Ruled by Her Prudent Love in Many Things"

That marriage is a good estate and one ordained by God is a truth that Christians have never explicitly denied. Yet there have been periods in the history of the church when there has been definitely been a low regard for this vital institution. The fourth-century theologian Jerome (c. 347–420), for instance, who was responsible for the Latin translation of the Bible known as the Vulgate, vigorously defended the view that celibacy was a vastly superior state to marriage, more virtuous, more pleasing to God. In Jerome's thinking, all those in the Scriptures closest to God were celibate. In fact, Jerome argued, sexual relations between spouses were a distinct obstacle to leading a life devoted to the pursuit of genuine spirituality.[2]

Augustine (354–430), another Latin-speaking theologian from

the same era, whose thought provided the foundation for much of the thinking of the Middle Ages, similarly maintained that the celibate individual who devotes himself or herself to Christ is like the angels and experiences a foretaste of heaven, for in heaven there is no marriage.[3] Why, then, did God ordain marriage? In Augustine's eyes, it was primarily for the procreation of children. Commenting on Genesis 2, Augustine was convinced that Eve would have been no use to Adam if she had not been able to bear children. What, then, of the biblical idea, found in this very chapter of Genesis, that the woman was made to be a delightful companion to the man, a source of comfort and strength? And what of the man as this for the woman? These ideas receive scant attention in the theology of Augustine.[4] In other works, Augustine argues that God instituted marriage for basically three reasons: (1) for the sake of fidelity, that is, the avoidance of illicit sex; (2) for the purpose of procreation; and (3) as a symbol of the unity of those who would inherit the heavenly Jerusalem.[5] These positions of Jerome and Augustine were largely embraced by the mediaeval Roman Catholic Church.

Some Puritan Perspectives on Marriage

So it was that for many in western Europe, the Reformation was not only a rediscovery of the heart of the gospel and the way of salvation, as we saw in the previous chapter, but it was also a recovery of the full panoply of ideas in the Bible surrounding marriage. After the death of his wife, Idelette, in March of 1549, John Calvin, for example, wrote to his fellow Reformer Pierre Viret (1511–1571), "I am deprived of my excellent life companion, who, if misfortune had come, would have been my willing companion not only in exile and sorrow, but even in death."[6] This simple statement from one of the central figures in the Reformation, who was normally very discreet about his personal feelings, is a doorway into Reformation thinking about marriage—its innate excellence, its importance as a place of Christian affection and friendship, its role as a school of sanctification. The Puritans, heirs to the Reformers in this as in so many other things, faithfully transmitted this teaching about marriage, but also, as J. I. Packer puts it, gave it "such strength, substance, and solidity as to warrant the verdict that . . . under God . . . they were creators of the English Christian marriage."[7]

Like the Reformers, the Puritans strongly opposed clerical celibacy and affirmed that marriage is as intrinsically good as virginity, even hinting that it might be better. As Thomas Adams (fl. 1612–1653), a renowned Puritan preacher in the mid-seventeenth century, put it: "There is no such fountain of comfort on earth, as marriage."[8] Similarly the Elizabethan Puritan author Robert Cleaver (died c. 1613) could state: "There can be no greater society or company, than is between a man and his wife."[9] The Puritans were very aware that marriage has other goods beyond the avoidance of fornication and its attendant evils.

William Gouge (1578–1653), a leader among London Puritans and a key participant at the Westminster Assembly, could repeat Augustine's view that God intended marriage for the procreation of children, but, he went on to emphasize, God also meant it for the mutual aid of husband and wife. "No such help," writes Gouge, "can man have from any other creature as from a wife; or a woman, as from an husband."[10] As the Puritans reflected on Genesis 2 they disagreed profoundly with Augustine's reading of the text. God made Eve to be far more than the bearer of Adam's children. She was to be his companion, for, as Cleaver noted: "The husband is also to understand, that as God created the woman, . . . so also he created her not of Adam's foot that she should be trodden down and despised, but he took her out of the rib, that she might walk jointly with him."[11] It is thus not fortuitous that when that quintessential Puritan text, the Westminster Confession of Faith, listed the reasons for marriage, this one of companionship comes in first place. "Marriage was ordained," we read in chapter 25.2, "for the mutual help of husband and wife, for the increase of mankind with a legitimate issue, and of the Church with an holy seed; and for preventing uncleanness."[12]

As Packer notes, Puritan preachers and authors are regularly "found pulling out the stops to proclaim the supreme blessing of togetherness in marriage."[13] For instance, Richard Baxter (1615–1691), whose experience of marriage with Margaret Charlton (1636–1681) will form the subject for the rest of this chapter, could state:

> It is a mercy to have a faithful friend, that loveth you entirely, and is as true to you as yourself, to whom you may open your mind and communicate your affairs, and who would be ready to strengthen you, and divide the cares of your affairs and family with you, and help you to bear your burdens, and comfort you in your sorrows, and be the daily companion of your lives, and partaker of your joys and sorrows. And it is a mercy to have so near a friend to be a helper to your soul; to join with you in prayer and other holy exercises; to watch over you and tell you of your sins and dangers, and to stir up in you the grace of God, and remember to you of the life to come, and cheerfully accompany you in the ways of holiness.[14]

Here Baxter speaks from rich and joyful experience. These words come from *A Christian Directory: or, A Sum of Practical Theology, and Cases of Conscience*, a "million-word compendium of Puritan teaching about Christian life and conduct,"[15] and were written in the mid-1660s, though the book was not published in its entirety until 1673. A few years before Baxter wrote these words he had married Margaret Charlton, one of his parishioners. Twentieth-century Baxter scholar N. H. Keeble well sums up their marriage: "Never minister had a better comrade. . . . When all is said, it must have been, except that it was a childless union, as near an 'ideal marriage' as may be hoped of man and woman."[16]

Richard and Margaret before Their Marriage[17]

The life of Richard Baxter spans much of the seventeenth century, one of the most decisive and turbulent eras of English history. Baxter grew up in Shropshire, not far from Shrewsbury. As a boy and a teen, his formal schooling was negligible, which is noteworthy in view of the fact that Baxter is considered to be one of the most learned of the Puritan divines. He appears to have obtained his education primarily through reading, which was also one of the major means God used to bring him to a saving knowledge of Christ. Later, looking back as a mature Christian on the time of his conversion, he would state that he did not know when it actually took place, a fact that made him somewhat uneasy. Further reflection, though, led him to realize that "God breaketh not all men's hearts alike."[18]

Another formative influence on his Christian life was chronic ill health that dogged him from his childhood. In 1671, when he was fifty-six, he recalled that from the age of fourteen "I have not been a year free from suffering, and since twenty two but few days, and since 1646 (which is about twenty five years), I have had but few hours free from pain (though through God's grace not intolerable)."[19] He was, in J. I. Packer's words, "a veritable museum of disease."[20] What was the effect of all this ill health? First, it accustomed Baxter to think of himself as a man on the verge of eternity. This perspective gave him, in his words, "a deep sense of time's great preciousness."[21] Then his physical problems produced in him a serious outlook on life. "The face of death, and nearness of eternity, did much convince me, what books to read, what studies to prefer and prosecute, what company and conversation to choose!"[22] Finally, it made him a serious and earnest preacher. "I preach'd," he once remarked in an oft-quoted aphorism, "as never sure to preach again and as a dying man to dying men."[23]

At the age of twenty-three, in 1638, Baxter was ordained a deacon. For the next two years he served as the curate or assistant to the Anglican minister at Bridgnorth, Shropshire, a man by the name of William Medstard. He then moved roughly thirteen miles south to Kidderminster, Worcestershire. This was the site of his most famous ministry, which took place between the years

1641 and 1661. When he arrived in the town, the vast bulk of its inhabitants were, in Baxter's own words, "an ignorant, rude and revelling people,"[24] but this was to change dramatically. The face and soul of the entire community was revolutionized as a result of Baxter's preaching once a Sunday and once on Thursday, his holding a weekly pastor's forum for theological discussion and prayer in which all of his people could participate, his distribution of Bibles and good Christian books, and his personal catechizing of the eight hundred families in the town on an annual basis.

Baxter can best tell us the dramatic results of this ministry.

> The congregation was usually full, so that we were fain to build five galleries after my coming thither, the church itself being very capacious [it held up to a thousand people], and the most commodious and convenient that ever I was in. Our private meetings also were full. On the Lord's-days there was no disorder to be seen in the streets, but you might hear an hundred families singing psalms and repeating sermons as you passed through the streets. In a word, when I came thither first there was about one family in a street that worshipped God and called on his name, and when I came away there were some streets where there was not passed one family in the side of a street that did not do so, and that did not, by professing serious godliness, give us hope of their sincerity.[25]

And the fruit of this ministry appears to have been genuine. It is fascinating to read a note that George Whitefield (1714–1770), the great evangelist of the eighteenth century, recorded in his diary on the last day of 1743 after a visit to Kidderminster: "I was greatly refreshed to find what a sweet savour of good Mr. Baxter's doctrine, works, and discipline remained to this day."[26]

Now, among those converted under Baxter's preaching at Kidderminster was Margaret Charlton. Like Baxter she came from Shropshire—she had, in fact, been raised only a few miles from where Baxter grew up, though in considerably wealthier circumstances. She came to live in Kidderminster with her godly mother, Mary Hanmer (d. 1661), who had been twice widowed and was delighting in Baxter's pulpit ministry. Initially, Margaret had little liking for either Baxter or the people of the town. She had, Baxter tells us in *A Breviate of the Life of Margaret, The Daughter of Francis Charlton, . . . and Wife of Richard Baxter*, his account of their lives together, a "great aversion to the poverty and strictness of the people" of the town. Frivolous and held by the gaieties of this world, she was far more interested in "glittering herself in costly apparel."[27]

The Holy Spirit, though, was at work in her life. A series of sermons that Baxter preached on the doctrine of conversion, which eventually found its way into print as *A Treatise of Conversion* (1657), was, Baxter tells us, "received on her heart as the seal on the wax." Her spiritual transformation was swift and genuine. As she later wrote:

> God hath . . . engaged me to himself, by taking me into his family, and planting me in his garden, and watering me with the dew from heaven. . . . I am thine, Lord, and not mine own. . . . Thou Lord that knowest all things, knowest that I have devoted my all to thee.[28]

One of the first signs of this radical change in her life was "her fervent, secret prayers." She chose to pray in a portion of her mother's house that was not in use since it had been damaged during the Civil Wars. She naturally thought she could not be heard. But her praying was overheard by her mother and friends in the house. According to Baxter, they said, "They never heard so fervent prayers from any person."[29]

Not long after her conversion, which brought much rejoicing to many in the town, she was stricken with consumption, and for a number of months her life seemed to be ebbing away. Baxter and a group of those whom he calls "humble praying persons" resolved to fast and pray for Margaret's healing. And God heard their prayers. The Lord, Baxter tells us, "speedily delivered her as it were by nothing."[30] At a public occasion in April 1660 when thanksgiving was made to God for her healing, Margaret acknowledged his great mercy to her, and she declared that she was "taking him only for my God and my chief felicity."[31]

The Historical Context

At the time of this dramatic reversal of Margaret's ambitions and goals in life, there were also great changes sweeping the national scene. Oliver Cromwell (1599–1658), who had become the ruler of a republican England in the 1650s after nearly ten years of religious civil war, had died two years previously. During the British Civil Wars the king, Charles I (1600–1649), had been executed as a traitor for making war on his own subjects, and his son, who would become Charles II (1630–1685), had been forced to flee into exile on the European continent. After Cromwell's death England seemed to be collapsing into anarchy, and the fateful decision was made by a number of Cromwell's former comrades-in-arms to restore the monarchy. Charles II stepped ashore at Dover on May 25, 1660, to a thunderous welcome. He was handed an English Bible, which he described as that which he loved more than anything else in the world. Subsequent events would cast doubt upon the sincerity of this profession.

Coming to power with Charles was a parliament bent on breaking forever the political power and spiritual influence of Puritanism. Those who had signed the death warrant of Charles I and were still surviving were quickly brought to trial and executed. The year after the restoration of the monarchy saw the first of a series of punitive measures against the Puritans, which would become known as the "Clarendon Code." Named after Charles's chief minister, they were aimed at all who would not conform completely to the rites of the Church of England. Particularly noteworthy is the Act of Uniformity, which came into effect on August 24, 1662. Roughly two thousand ministers were ejected from their ministries because they would not give unfeigned assent to everything in the *Book of Common Prayer*, which ordered the worship life of the Church of England. Among them was Baxter.

His precious ministry at Kidderminster was taken from him and it was now illegal for him to preach or lead in worship not only there but also anywhere in England. Shining in this time of darkness was "one brilliant shaft of light"[32]—his marriage to Margaret, just over two weeks after the Act of Uniformity took effect.

Richard and Margaret: The Shape of Their Marriage

For various reasons the marriage of Richard and Margaret became the talk of London. There was the difference in their ages, Richard being old enough to be her father. Then there was the disparity in their social station, her mother's death in 1661 having given her considerable wealth. Finally, it was common knowledge that Baxter had advocated celibacy for ministers, due to their need to devote themselves unreservedly to their ministries.[33] While Baxter never affirmed the Roman Catholic view that the marriage of pastors was unlawful, he did caution those with a desire to oversee a flock:

> The work of the sacred ministry is enough to take up the whole man, if he had the strength and parts of many men. . . . Believe it, he that will have a wife must spend much of his time in her conference, prayer, and other family duties. . . . And if he have children, O how much care, time and labour they will require.[34]

Once he was married, though, Baxter found that marriage agreed with him very well. As he wrote after his wife's death: "We lived in inviolated love and mutual complacency sensible of the benefit of mutual help. These near nineteen years I know not that we ever had any breach in the point of love, or point of interest."[35]

Now, this statement needs to be read in light of the fact that neither Richard nor Margaret was an easygoing individual.

Richard, a scholar and something of a recluse, was unpolished in social graces. He could be testy and his tongue sharp, a possible side effect of regularly living in pain.[36] Margaret would gently scold him when he was careless or rash in his speech. Writes Baxter, "If my very looks seemed not pleasant, she would have me amend them (which my weak and pained state of body undisposed me to do)."[37] Baxter learned a valuable lesson about marriage through Margaret's correction of his faults. It was nothing less than a school of sanctification. As he advised husbands and wives in his *Christian Directory*:

> Conceal not the state of your souls, nor hide your faults from one another. You are as one flesh, and should have one heart: and as it is most dangerous for a man to be unknown to himself, so is it very hurtful to husband or wife to be unknown to one another, in those cases wherein they have need of help. It is foolish tenderness of yourselves, when you conceal your disease from your physician, or your helpful friend; and who should be so tender of you, and helpful to you, as you should be to one another? Indeed in some few cases, where the opening of a fault or secret will but tend to quench affection, and not to get assistance from another, it is wisdom to conceal it; but that is not the ordinary case. The opening your hearts to each other is necessary to your mutual help.[38]

Margaret, on the other hand, was often overwhelmed by obsessive irrational fears, nightmares, and dread. Some of it was undoubtedly caused by nearly dying at least four times before she ever met Richard as well as by an especially traumatic incident in the Civil War, when her mother's castle was besieged, taken, and sacked, and "men lay killed before her face."[39] And she too wrestled with a number of physical complaints, in particular, regular bouts of migraine and congestion of the lungs.[40] Moreover, she had "an extraordinary sharp and piercing wit," and was able to size up the character of men and women fairly quickly. She tended,

Baxter tells us, to be quiet and reserved, and given her gift of understanding others, expected "all should know her mind without [her] expressing it." Not surprisingly, when people, including her husband, failed to understand what she was thinking, she felt frustrated.[41] Yet, unlike her husband, she had no struggles with anger.

Moreover, the circumstances in which they had been raised gave them quite different expectations about how to keep house, which undoubtedly caused some tension. Baxter writes of himself:

> I had been bred among plain, mean [that is, humble] people, and I thought that so much washing of stairs and rooms, to keep them as clean as their trenchers and dishes and so much ado about cleanliness and trifles, was sinful curiosity, and expense of servants' time, who might that while have been reading some good book. But she that was otherwise bred had somewhat other thoughts.[42]

Years alone had made Baxter oblivious to the affairs of running a household. Eventually, though, he was happy to have one so efficient manage his affairs.

The Baxter household, like all but the poorest of the time, had servants. Margaret proved to be an extremely kind and caring mistress to them, almost always overlooking their faults and mistakes.[43] She insisted that Richard catechize them once a week and teach them from the Bible. On occasion Baxter would be so caught up in his studies that he would forget this duty. Margaret would then gently remind him with an expression of "trouble" on her face.[44] Servants in the Baxter home were treated as family: "She had an earnest desire of the conversion and salvation of her servants," Baxter wrote, "and was greatly troubled that so many of them (although tolerable in their work) went away ignorant, or strange to true godliness, as they came; and such as were truly converted with us she loved as children."[45]

They also lived in very difficult times when those known as Puritans found themselves tossed into a furnace of persecution.

Richard, known as a key leader among the Puritans, was dogged by spies, the frequent object of slander, and on at least one occasion arrested and imprisoned. They had to move house frequently and more than once lived in what could only be called wretched circumstances.[46] One gets a good idea of the nature of Margaret's mettle when Baxter tells us that at the time of his first imprisonment in 1669, Margaret "cheerfully went with me into prison; she brought her best bed thither, and did much to remove the removable inconveniences of the prison. I think she scarce ever had a pleasanter time in her life than while she was with me there."[47]

"The Meetest Helper I Could Have Had"[48]

As one reads Richard's account of his marriage, there is little doubt of his and Margaret's deep respect for one another and their unbounded appreciation of one another's gifts and strengths. Baxter freely admitted that Margaret was better than he at solving problems relating to financial and civil affairs. "She would at the first hearing," he wrote, "understand the matter better than I could do by many and long thoughts."[49] Even when it came to practical issues of the Christian life, Baxter came to lean on his wife's wisdom.

> Her apprehension of such things was so much quicker, and more discerning than mine, that though I was naturally somewhat tenacious of my own conceptions, her reasons and my experience usually told me she was in the right, and knew more than I. She would at the first hearing understand the matter better than I could do by many and long thoughts. . . . Yes, I will say that . . . except in cases that required learning and skill in theological difficulties, she was better at resolving a case of conscience than most divines that ever I knew in all my life. I often put cases to her, which she suddenly so resolved, as to convince me of some degree of oversight in my own resolution. Insomuch that of late years, I confess, that I was used to put all, save secret cases, to her and hear what she could say. . . . And

she would lay all the circumstances presently together, compare them, and give me a more exact resolution than I could do. [50]

Thus, Richard could state: "I am not ashamed to have been much ruled by her prudent love in many things."[51] As Bo Salisbury rightly notes, Richard's marriage to Margaret "reveals still another facet in Baxter's exceptional abilities as a shepherd and one which modern pastors may want to pay particular attention to; his spirit of humility and submission to others. With men, the relationship with their wives will often reveal the depth or shallowness of their humility and so, their suitability to the task of humble, servant leadership within the Body of Christ."[52]

Margaret, in turn, recognized Richard's giftedness as a preacher. Despite the fact that it was illegal for him to preach, she regularly used large portions of her wealth to secure rooms in London where he could preach. She even went so far as to pay for chapels to be built for her husband's ministry. One instance that Baxter particularly recalled took place in 1673:

> At London, when she saw me too dull and backward to seek any employment till I was called . . . she first fisht out of me in what place I most desired more preaching. I told her in St. Martin's Parish, where are said to be forty thousand more than can come into the Church . . . where neighbors many live like Americans, and have heard no Sermon of many years.[53]

So she rented a large upstairs room where Baxter could preach on Sunday mornings and another minister could preach in the evening. During the very first meeting, the crowd of people who had come to hear Baxter was so great—there were close to eight hundred—that the floor beam gave out a loud crack and then another, which "set them all on running, and crying out at the windows for ladders." Margaret Baxter pushed her way downstairs through the crowd and the first man she met, she asked what his profession was. He turned out to be a carpenter. He lived close by, and so he went and fetched a suitable prop for the beam. The next day they pulled up the flooring and found the beam was held by so slender a piece of wood that they "took it for a wonder that the house fell not suddenly." The building obviously could not contain the crowds attracted by Baxter's preaching. The fright of so many having nearly perished, Baxter noted, "increased my wife's diseased frightfulness; so that she never got all the effects of it while she lived."[54]

Not to be defeated, however, Margaret set out in 1676 to have a new chapel built from the ground up on a nearby vacant lot. Baxter preached the first Sunday after its completion, but was absent the following week since he had to travel to a place about twenty miles outside of London. Robert Seddon (1629–1695), a preacher from Derbyshire—"an humble pious man" is the way Baxter describes him—agreed to take Baxter's place and preach the next Lord's Day. State officials, though, had learned about the venture and were determined to arrest Baxter for illegal preaching. Getting a warrant for his arrest, they descended on the chapel. Not finding Baxter, though, they arrested Seddon in his stead and put him in prison for a number of months. Margaret felt Seddon's imprisonment keenly and blamed herself. Thus, she used her own funds to visit and comfort him in the prison, pay all of his lawyer's fees, and also support his family.[55]

There was a cost to all this labor, and it was not merely material. It also brought, Richard writes, "trouble of body and mind; for her knife was too keen and cut the sheath. Her desires were more earnestly set on doing good, than her tender mind and head could well bear."[56] There were some, coming from the position that a woman's place is primarily in the home, who blamed Margaret for busying "her head so much about churches, and works of charity" and not being "content to live privately and quietly."[57] But Baxter defended her:

> This is but just what profane unbelievers say against all zeal and spiritual godliness: what needs there all this ado? Doth

not Paul call some women his helps in the gospel?[58] He that knows what it is to do good, and makes it the business of his life in the world, and knows what it is to give account of our stewardship, and to be doomed as the unprofitable slothful servant, will know how to answer this accusation.[59]

Some Concluding Thoughts

Richard and Margaret, like every married couple, were imperfect characters. As Richard said: "My dear wife did look for more good in me than she found, especially lately in my weakness and decay. We are all like pictures that must not be looked at too near. They that come near us find more faults and badness in us than others at a distance know."[60] And although the very trying circumstances in which they lived out their lives were more stressful than those that face most couples, all couples experience tension and stress. Yet, they managed to have a wonderful marriage. What was their secret?

Well, two things in particular stand out. First, Richard and Margaret followed the advice that Richard gave to married couples in his *Christian Directory*:

Husband and wife must take delight in the love, and company, and converse of each other. There is nothing that man's heart is so inordinately set upon as delight; and yet the lawful delight allowed them by God, they can turn into loathing and disdain. The delight which would entangle you in sin, and turn you from your duty and from God, is that which is forbidden you: but this is a delight that is helpful to you in your duty, and would keep you from sin. When husband and wife take pleasure in each other, it uniteth them in duty, it helpeth them with ease to do their work, and bear their burdens; and is not the least part of the comfort of the married state. "Rejoice with the wife of thy youth, as the loving hind and pleasant roe, let her breast satisfy thee at all times, and be thou ravished always with her love" [Prov. 5:18–19].[61]

But most importantly they had a tremendous agreement about what ultimately mattered in this life. "Suitableness in religious judgment and disposition," Baxter wrote as he drew his account of his marriage to Margaret to a close,

> preserveth faster love and concord (as it did with us) than suitableness in age, education and wealth; but yet those should not be imprudently neglected. Nothing causeth so near and fast and comfortable an union as to be united in one God, one Christ, one Spirit, one Church, one hope of heavenly glory.[62]

3

Anne Dutton and
Her Theological Works

"The Glory of God, and the Good of Souls"

While women in the early modern era worked as tailors, milliners, shoemakers, embroiderers, brewers, and confectioners, even apothecaries and blacksmiths, the professions of teacher, lawyer, and doctor, all of which required education, were closed to them. Nor were women encouraged to be authors. When Anne Locke Prowse (1530–after 1590), the wife of the Puritan Edward Dering (d. 1576), for example, published her translation of *Of the markes of the children of God* by Jean Taffin (1529–1602), the Walloon minister and theologian, she stated in her dedicatory letter:

> Everyone in his calling is bound to do somewhat to the furtherance of the holy building; but because great things by reason of my sex, I may not do, and that which I may, I ought to do, I have according to my duty, brought my poor basket

of stones to the strengthening of the walls of that Jerusalem, whereof (by grace) we are all both citizens and members.[1]

This attitude regarding female authors persisted well into the eighteenth century, as evidenced by Anne Dutton's (1692–1765) defense of her authorship in a small twelve-page tract, *A letter to such of the Servants of Christ, who may have any scruple about the Lawfulness of Printing any thing written by a Woman* (1743). The man of letters, Samuel Johnson (1709–1784), typical of male critics of female authors, considered women writers in this era to be "Amazons of the pen."[2] Against such a background, the literary legacy of Dutton becomes all the more significant.[3]

Biographical Sketch of Anne's Early Years

Dutton was born Anne Williams in Northampton to godly Congregationalist parents. Anne attended the Independent Congregational Church at Castle Hill, professing conversion at the age of thirteen and joining the church two years later under the pastorate of John Hunt (d. 1709). After Hunt's death Thomas Tingey became Williams's pastor in 1709, about whom Anne had little positive to say. Due to her dissatisfaction with his ministry, she moved to the open-membership Baptist church in College Lane, Northampton, a church in which membership was granted on profession of faith without the necessity of baptism. It was here, under the ministry of John Moore (d. 1726), that she was baptized as a believer and became an active member. There, in her words, she found "fat, green pastures," for "Mr. Moore was a great doctrinal preacher." As she went on to explain: "The special advantage I received under his ministry, was the establishment of my judgement in the doctrines of the gospel."[4]

When she was twenty-two, in 1714, she married Thomas Cattell, and moved with her husband to London. While there she worshiped with the Calvinistic Baptist church that met at premises on Wood Street within Cripplegate. Founded by Hanserd Knollys

(1599–1691), one of the leading Baptist figures of the seventeenth century, this work had known some rough times in the days immediately before Anne and Thomas came to the church. David Crosley (1670–1744), the evangelist of the Pennines, had been the pastor of the work from 1705 to 1709, but he had been disfellowshiped for drunkenness, unchaste conduct with women, and lying to the church about these matters when accused. He would, many years later, know some usefulness again in the Lord's work.[5] But in the 1710s he had lost all credibility. The sorrow and sense of betrayal, disappointment, and consternation in the church must have run deep.

It was not until 1714 that the church succeeded in finding a new pastor. John Skepp (1675–1721), a member of the Cambridge Congregationalist church of Joseph Hussey (1659–1726), was called that year to be the pastor. Now, Hussey is often seen as the father of the theological error of hyper-Calvinism, insomuch as he argued in his book *God's Operations of Grace: but No Offers of Grace* (1707) that offering Christ indiscriminately to sinners is something that dishonors the Holy Spirit for it smacks of "creature-co-operation and creature-concurrence" in the work of salvation.[6] Skepp published but one book, and that appeared posthumously: *Divine Energy: or The Efficacious Operations of the Spirit of God upon the Soul of Man* (1722). In it he appears to have followed Hussey's approach to evangelism. It is sometimes argued that Anne Dutton's exposure to hyper-Calvinism at a young age shaped her thinking for the rest of her life. If so, it is curious to find her rejoicing in the ministry of preachers such as George Whitefield in later years.

Skepp, though, was an impressive preacher. The overall trend in the church during his ministry was one of growth. There were 179 members when he came as pastor in 1714. When he died in 1721, church membership had grown to 212. And Anne delighted in what she called his "quickness of thought, aptness of expression, suitable affection, and a most agreeable delivery."[7] In the early months of 1719, though, Anne's life underwent a deep trial as her husband of but five or six years died. She returned to her family in Northampton and found herself wrestling spiritually. In her words, Anne sought God "in ordinances, in one place and another; but alas! I found him not."[8] She was not long single though. A second marriage in the middle months of 1720 was to Benjamin Dutton (1691–1747), who was the youngest of six children of Matthew Dutton (d. 1719) and a clothier who had studied for vocational ministry in various places, among them Glasgow University. Anne and he had met in the final months of 1719, and within a year they were wed.[9]

Ministry took the couple to such towns as Whittlesey and Wisbech in Cambridgeshire, before leading them finally in 1731 to a Baptist congregation in Great Gransden, Huntingdonshire, about twelve and a half miles due east of Cambridge. It is noteworthy that prior to this call to Great Gransden, Benjamin Dutton had wrestled with alcoholism. But the Lord delivered him completely around this time. In Benjamin Dutton's own words:

> The time of my deliverance being come, as was said, the Lord drew very near to my spirit: Set my heart against sin, all sin, and particularly against *that* sin which had been my great wound. And I was firmly resolved, by the Lord's help, that I would keep at the greatest distance from every, even the least, appearance of that evil, in a particular manner.[10]

And again he said that he now "stood not in need of wine, or strong drink. The Lord also, of his great goodness, took away my *inclination* thereto; so that I had no more inclination to it, or desire after it, than if I had never tasted any in my whole life."[11]

Under Dutton's preaching the church flourished so that on any given Sunday the congregation numbered anywhere between 250 and 350, of whom roughly fifty were members. This growth led to the building of a new meetinghouse, which can still be seen in the village. Benjamin perished at sea, however, in 1747. He had gone to America to help raise funds to pay off the debt incurred in the building of the meetinghouse, and the ship on which he was returning foundered not far from the British coast. Widowed now for the second time, Anne was to live another eighteen years. During that time "the fame of her primitive piety," to use the way that Baptist historian Joseph Ivimey (1773–1834) referred to her New Testament–like spirituality, became known in evangelical circles on both sides of the Atlantic and that through various literary publications.

A Talent for Writing

Anne had been writing for a number of years before Benjamin's demise. After his death a steady stream of tracts and treatises, collections of selected correspondence, and poems poured from her pen. Among her numerous correspondents were Howel Harris (1714–1773); Selina Hastings, the Countess of Huntingdon (1707–1791); and George Whitefield—all of them key figures in the eighteenth-century Evangelical Revival that was sweeping through the English-speaking world in the mid-eighteenth century. After the expulsion of the Puritans from the Church of England in 1662, as noted in the previous chapter, the Puritan cause had splintered into three major groups: the Presbyterians, the Congregationalists, and the Particular or Calvinistic Baptists. Anne Dutton belonged to this third community. Along with the Church of England, all three of these bodies experienced significant decline in the early decades of the eighteenth century. The English Presbyterians essentially lost their grip on classical orthodoxy and became Unitarians. The Congregationalists and Particular Baptists retained the core doctrines of the Christian faith but stagnated for a variety of reasons and were recognizably in deep need of revival or renewal by the middle of the eighteenth century.

When revival did come in the 1730s, it started among the Anglicans. This was a shock to the Congregationalists and Baptists, for was it not their communities that had retained the faith and especially the biblical form of church governance—namely, a congregational model—after going through the fires of persecution in the second half of the seventeenth century? Many Congregationalists and Baptists were thus deeply suspicious of the authenticity of the revival. It is noteworthy that Anne Dutton built close relationships with many of the key figures of the revival in the early days of the awakening.

Howel Harris was convinced that the Lord had entrusted her "with a talent of writing for him." When William Seward (1711–1740), an early Methodist preacher who was killed by a mob in Wales, read a letter she had written to him in May 1739, he found it "full of such comforts and direct answers to what I had been writing that it filled my eyes with tears of joy." And Whitefield, who helped promote and publish Anne's writings, said after meeting her that "her conversation is as weighty as her letters."[12]

By 1740 she had written seven books; fourteen more followed between 1741 and 1743. Yet another fourteen had been published by 1750.[13] In fact, she continued to write up until her death in 1765. Without children of her own, she came to regard her fifty or so books as her offspring. She was clearly the most prolific female Baptist author of the eighteenth century.

But she wrestled with whether it was biblical for her to be an authoress. In her tract *A letter to such of the Servants of Christ, who may have any scruple about the Lawfulness of Printing any thing written by a Woman*, Dutton maintained that she wrote not for fame but for "only the glory of God, and the good of souls."[14] To those who might accuse her of violating 1 Timothy 2:12, she answered that her books were not intended to be read in a public setting of worship, which the 1 Timothy text was designed to address. Rather, the instruction that her books gave was private, for they were read by believers in "their own private houses."[15] She asked those who opposed women writers to "imagine then . . . when my books come to your house, that I am come to give you a visit" and to "patiently attend" to her infant "lispings."[16] What if some other authoresses had used the press for "trifles"? Well, she answered, "shall none of that sex be suffered to appear on Christ's side, to tell of the wonders of his love, to seek the good of souls, and the advancement of the Redeemer's interest?"[17]

On Christian Perfection

Anne was not slow to critique theological positions she felt erroneous. For instance, she was critical of the Sandemanians, who promoted an intellectualist faith,[18] and of William Romaine (1714–1795), a leading figure in the Evangelical Revival, whom she criticized for his view of the Godhead—she suspected him of being a modalist.[19] She was also a critic of John Wesley (1703–1791) and his brand of evangelical Arminianism, though her criticism was never abusive. In addition to a number of letters to Wesley, she wrote two booklets critiquing Wesley: first, a defense of Calvinism, *A Letter to the Reverend Mr. John Wesley, in Vindication of the Doctrines of Absolute, unconditional Election, Particular Redemption, Special Vocation, and Final Perseverance* (1742); and then the following year, an attack on Wesley's teaching about Christian perfection, *Letters to the Reverend Mr. John Wesley against Perfection as Not Attainable in this Life* (1743).[20] Around the time that she wrote the second of these tracts, she sent *A Letter from Mrs. Anne Dutton to The Reverend Mr. G. Whitefield* (1743), which Whitefield had printed in Philadelphia by the well-known printer William Bradford (1719–1791), the publisher of *The Pennsylvania Journal*.[21]

In the early 1740s John Wesley had begun to teach in London and Bristol that Christian perfection—the absence of known sin and complete love to God and man—was possible in this life as a post-conversion experience. Wesley referred to this experience as the "second blessing." Yet, true to his Arminianism, Wesley maintained that this state could be lost. Not surprisingly, some of Wesley's followers went one step further and affirmed that once experienced, this blessing could not be lost for the very fact that the possibility of sinning had been removed by the blessing. In the tract to Whitefield, Dutton first laid out her concern:

> O poor Bristol! How have many there been deluded by sin and Satan, in such a manner, as to think they have no sin. For indeed sir, I can look upon it to be no other than a delusion of the enemy of souls, and a deceit of the heart, for any to think, that there is such a thing attainable in this life, as an entire, sinless perfection; and much more so, for any to think, that they themselves have attained it. Strange it is, that any should think, or affirm, that they have not sinned in thought, word or deed for months! And stranger still, and what I never before heard of, that any should imagine that the being of sin is taken out of their nature![22]

For Anne, "entire, sinless perfection" is a satanic delusion. She lost no time in rubbishing this view on the basis of a number of Scripture texts, of which the most significant one for her was Titus 2:11–12:

> "If we say that we have no sin," (says the Apostle John) "we deceive ourselves, and the truth is not in us," 1 John 1:8. And says the Holy Ghost by Solomon, "there is not a just man upon the earth that doeth good, and sinneth not," Eccles 7:20. The great work of the grace of God, which bringeth salvation to the saved ones is teaching them, that denying "ungodliness and worldly lusts, they should live soberly, righteously, and godly in this present world," Titus 2:11, 12. The word *teaching*, being in the present tense, denotes the constant work of divine grace upon the subjects thereof, while they are in this world. The word *denying*, denotes the constant duty, and business of Christians, so long as they are in this present world. And the teaching of grace to deny ungodliness, and the denying of the same, both being of equal duration with the stay of Christians in this present world: do necessarily imply, the being, and solicitations of ungodliness, and worldly lusts in their souls, even so

long as they are in the body, or in this present world. To deny a person or thing supposes the being and solicitations of that person or thing. So to deny ungodliness and worldly lusts supposes the being, and solicitations thereof. And as a Christian's work, his constant work, lies in a continual denying of ungodliness, and worldly lusts; it must undeniably suppose the being, and solicitations of sin, so long as they are in this world.[23]

Here, Anne initially appeals to 1 John 1:8 and Ecclesiastes 7:20 to argue for the reality of sin in the life of every human being in this world. Her main text is Titus 2:11–12, where she argues that the present tense of the main verbs in this verse, "teaching" and "denying," imply an ever-present duty in the believer's life, which must mean that he or she is never free from sin in this world.

Anne finds further support for her position in 2 Corinthians 7:1 and 1 John 3:2–3:

2 Cor. 7.1 "having these promises (dearly beloved) let us cleanse ourselves from all filthiness of the flesh and spirit", perfecting holiness in the fear of God: doth necessarily suppose our present impurity and imperfection, both in the soul and body, while in this life. So also, 1 John 3.3, "And every man that hath this hope in him, purifieth himself, even as he is pure"; doth necessarily imply his present *impurity* while he is in this world; (or until he enjoys the hoped for blessing, of seeing Christ as he is) else there would be no room to say of him, that he *purifies* himself. So likewise, our *imperfection* in holiness, which arises from the being, and working of sin in our corrupt nature, is necessarily implied, ver. 2, where the Apostle says, "When he shall appear, we shall be like him; for we shall see him as he is." He doth not say we *are* like him; . . . but we *shall* be like him. And [he] gives the great cause of this great effect: for we shall *see* him as he is. *Sight* of Christ is the cause of likeness to him. Sight of Christ *partial* in this life produceth *partial* likeness. Sight of Christ *total* in the life to come will produce *total* likeness to him.[24]

Again, Anne carefully looked at these biblical texts and found that both support the idea that perfect holiness is a reality of the life to come, not life in this world. Her final remarks are pithy and reminiscent of Puritan preaching, which often contained pithy remarks as a teaching tool: "Sight of Christ *partial* in this life produceth *partial* likeness. Sight of Christ *total* in the life to come will produce *total* likeness to him."

The Presence of the Lord Christ at the Lord's Supper

One of Anne's most important writings, valuable for its eucharistic piety, is her *Thoughts on the Lord's Supper, Relating to the Nature, Subjects, and right Partaking of this Solemn Ordinance*, which was published anonymously in 1748. As we noted in chapter 1, one of the most divisive issues between the Roman Catholic Church and the Reformers as well as between the Reformers themselves was over the nature of the presence of Christ at the Table. While all of the Reformers rejected the Roman dogma of transubstantiation, they were not agreed about what actually happens during the celebration of the Lord's Supper.

In the view of Martin Luther (1483–1546), Christ's body and blood are present "in, with and under" the bread and the wine. Contrary to the Roman dogma of transubstantiation, the bread remains bread; yet, in some way, it also actually contains Christ's body after the prayer of consecration. Likewise the wine contains his blood after this prayer, though it remains wine. The Swiss Reformer Huldreich Zwingli (1484–1531), on the other hand, regarded the bread and the wine as mainly signs of what God has accomplished through the death of Christ and the Supper therefore as chiefly a memorial. In recent discussions of Zwingli's perspective on the Lord's Supper it is often maintained that Zwingli was not really a Zwinglian; that is, he saw more in the Lord's Supper than simply a memorial.[25] Whatever Zwingli's position, a tradition did take its start from those aspects of his thought that stressed primarily the memorial nature of the Lord's Supper.

A third view that sought to strike a *via media* between those of Luther and Zwingli and prevent a permanent estrangement between the Lutherans and Zwinglians was that of John Calvin (1509–1564). In Calvin's perspective on the nature of the Lord's Supper, the bread and wine are signs and guarantees of a present reality. To the one who eats the bread and drinks the wine with faith, there is conveyed what they symbolize, namely Christ. The channel, as it were, through which Christ is conveyed to the believer is none other than the Holy Spirit. The Spirit acts as a kind of link or bridge between believers and the ascended Christ. Christ is received by believers in the Supper, "not because Christ inheres the elements, but because the Holy Spirit binds believers" to him. But without faith, only the bare elements are received.[26]

Anne's *Thoughts on the Lord's Supper* is one of the better eighteenth-century expositions of Calvin's view. Dutton devotes the first section of her sixty-page treatise on the Lord's Supper to outlining its nature. In this section Dutton argues that the Supper is, among other things, a "communication." "As our Lord is spiritually present in his own ordinance," she writes, "so he therein and thereby doth actually communicate, or give himself, his body broken, and his blood shed, with all the benefits of his death, to the worthy receivers."[27] Here Dutton is affirming that Christ is indeed present at the celebration of his Supper and makes it a means of grace for those who partake of it with faith. As she states later on in this treatise: in the Lord's Supper "the King is pleased to sit with us, at his Table."[28]

Her biblical proof is found in 1 Corinthians 10:16, which she has rightly interpreted as implying the presence of Christ at the Table. In this passage Paul is arguing that Christians should not believe that idol worship is harmless because pagan gods have no real existence in the world. In 1 Corinthians 8:5 Paul had stated that Graeco-Roman culture knew of "many 'gods' and many 'lords'" in heaven and on earth. But, the apostle goes on in the following verse, whatever his Greek and Roman contemporaries might believe, he and his fellow Christians were assured that there was but "one God, the Father" and "one Lord Jesus Christ." As for the Greek and Roman gods, the ancient church recognized that they had, in Paul's words, "no real existence" (1 Cor. 8:3). Undoubtedly they "existed" for those who worshiped them, but from the standpoint of reality they simply did not exist. They were, as Paul says in his speech on Mars Hill, a classic defense of the Christian perspective on life, "an image formed by the art and imagination of man" (Acts 17:29). Yet, Paul goes on to argue in 1 Corinthians 10, this did not mean that pagan religion was harmless. In fact, it was "the locus of demonic activity, and . . . to worship such "gods" is in fact to fellowship with demons" (1 Cor. 10:19–20).[29] And to illustrate his point that idol worship involves the presence of other beings besides the worshipers, Paul gives the example of temple worship in the Old Testament and the Lord's Supper. In the latter case, his argument assumes that worship at the Lord's Supper involves the presence of the Lord Jesus.

So highly does she prize this means of grace that she can state, with what other Calvinistic Baptists of her era might describe as some exaggeration, that the celebration of the Lord's Supper "admits" believers "into the nearest approach to his [i.e., Christ's] glorious self, that we can make in an ordinance-way on the Earth, on this side the presence of his glory in heaven."[30] Anne's language may sound extravagant to some, but it reveals, I believe, something of the spiritual intensity that was available to Baptist congregations in the mid-eighteenth century. In fact, one of the few negative effects of the Evangelical Revival may well be the way in which this spirituality of the Table was diluted in the press to make churches primarily centers for evangelism.

A Christ-centeredness and cross-centeredness permeate the entire treatise. To give but one example: "O what a wondrous draught," she declares near the beginning of the book, "what a life-giving draught, in his own most precious blood, doth God our

Saviour, the Lord our Lover, give to dying sinners, to his beloved ones in this glorious ordinance."[31]

Anne's Final Days

Anne died on Monday, November 17, 1765, probably from throat cancer. There is a powerful account of her final days from Robert Robinson (1735–1790), in a letter that he wrote to a friend in 1766 and that has only recently come to light.

> You have (no doubt) heard of Dear Mrs Dutton's departure. I saw her a few weeks before she died. She apprehended her death near then. She could not get into the meeting[house] at the sermon. . . . O how ravishingly she talked. She was up, and sat by the fire. Her countenance—I won't say serene and composed, but blithe[,] gay, full of a serenity, or rather full of immortality—my mind was full of that Scripture which I thought I then saw exemplified in Mrs. Dutton. Psal. 92.12 etc. *The righteous shall flourish like the palm–tree,* which it seems grows fastest under burdens. . . . *They shall still bring forth fruit in old age.*—A woman of seventy-four laden with the fruits of the spirit. *Love, joy, peace, longsuffering, gentleness, goodness, faith, meekness, temperance.* Gal. 5.22. . . . Not shriveled, wrinkled, nor spotted with doubts, fears, deadness, etc., but like fine ripe fruits, at once charming the eye, refreshing the smell, & gratifying the tast[e]. The sight answered the end mentioned by the Psalmist. . . . I had heard, that precious in the sight of the Lord was the *death* of his saints, and now I saw he [i.e., God] was true to his word, for he was present by his Spirit in the sickness and death of Mrs. Dutton. Her illness was a sore throat, and one of her expressions was, "My dear Sir, I am rejoiced to think that there is but a hair's breadth betwixt me and my father's house. 'Tis but for God to stop my breath and I am with him. And so shall I be ever with the Lord."[32]

4

Sarah Edwards and
the Vision of God

"A Wonderful Sweetness"

Like all revivals, the First Great Awakening of the eighteenth century was not an idyllic event: in addition to great blessing, there were problems. In this case, it was incidents and patterns of fanaticism. The key theologian who addressed these matters was the New England author Jonathan Edwards (1703–1758).[1] Among his defenses of the revival is his *Some Thoughts concerning the present Revival of Religion in New-England*, which was written during the course of 1742, although it was not actually published till mid-March 1743.[2] During the period of time that Edwards devoted to writing it, a division over the revival was becoming increasingly obvious. Two parties were emerging, the Old Lights and the New Lights, as they came to be called, which, Edwards observes, had the tendency to divide the churches in New England into "two armies, separated, drawn up in battle array, ready to fight with one another."[3] In an attempt to bring peace to this situation, Edwards drew up this lengthy work, which ran to 378 pages in its first edition.

While Edwards was committed to supporting the revival as an authentic work of God the Holy Spirit, he was increasingly critical of the imprudent excesses committed by certain "friends" of the revival.[4] The book is divided into five main parts. In the first part the Northampton pastor defends the revival as a "glorious work of God."[5] The next division of the book outlines the "obligations that all are under to acknowledge, rejoice in, and promote this work."[6] The third section seeks to vindicate the "zealous promoters" of this work.[7] The largest part of the book is part 4, which focuses on how the friends of the revival need to correct various problems in the work.[8] The final section is devoted to outlining various things that could be done to further promote the revival.[9] The length of the fourth part of the book makes it abundantly clear that Edwards's growing concern is the very real danger of fanaticism. "One truly zealous person," he observes, "may do more (through Satan's being too subtle for him) to hinder the work, than an hundred great, and strong, and open opposers."[10] Now, one aspect of the work that is unique and noteworthy is the account of Sarah Edwards's (1710–1758) spiritual experience in which Edwards presents his wife as a model of a truly Spirit-filled person.[11]

Sarah Pierpont through Jonathan Edwards's Eyes

Amanda Porterfield has noted, in a recent historical study of the spirituality of American women:

> One of the most striking phenomena about the New England Puritans is that their greatest ministers and governors—Thomas Shepard, John Winthrop, Simon Bradstreet, Edward Taylor, and Jonathan Edwards, for example—loved their wives beyond measure. These men found their wives to be earthly representatives of God's beauty. For these men a loving wife was not only a model Christian but also an expression of the beauty of the world that pointed beyond itself to divine

beauty. And the enjoyment of God's beauty was the essence of Puritan spirituality.[12]

The few texts we have from the hand of Edwards that are explicitly about his wife, Sarah, certainly help to substantiate these striking remarks. Regretfully, Sarah was not a writer, and she did not leave behind her an extensive journal or substantial correspondence by which we might outline her spiritual life. But we do have a text about her early life that has just recently come to light, and there is the remarkable text in *Some Thoughts*, mentioned above, that provides an insight into the workings of her heart. For much of her life, though, we must rely on the words of others, especially those of her husband and his first biographer, Samuel Hopkins.

Sarah had been born into a family rich in spiritual privileges. Her father, James Pierpont (d. 1714), had been the minister of First Church, New Haven, Connecticut, from 1685 till his death. Her mother, Mary Hooker, was the granddaughter of Thomas Hooker (1586–1647), one of the most influential first-generation Puritans in New England. Jonathan met his future wife around 1723 when she was thirteen and he twenty. As he wrote about her:

They say there is a young lady in [New Haven] who is beloved of that almighty Being, who made and rules the world, and that there are certain seasons in which this Great Being, in some way or other invisible, comes to her and fills her mind with exceeding sweet delight, and that she hardly cares for any thing, except to meditate on him—that she expects after a while to be received up where he is, to be raised out of the world and caught up into heaven; being assured that he loves her too well to let her remain at a distance from him always. There she is to dwell with him, and to be ravished with his love, favor and delight forever. Therefore, if you present all the world before her, with the richest of its treasures, she disregards it and cares not for it, and is unmindful of any pain or affliction. She has a strange sweetness in her mind, and sweetness of temper, uncommon purity in her affections; is most just and praiseworthy in all her actions; and you could not persuade her to do anything thought wrong or sinful, if you would give her all the world, lest she should offend this great Being. She is of a wonderful sweetness, calmness and universal benevolence of mind; especially after those times in which this great God has manifested himself to her mind. She will sometimes go about, singing sweetly, from place to [place]; and she seems to be always full of joy and pleasure; and no one know for what. She loves to be alone, and to wander in the fields and on the mountains, and seems to have someone invisible always conversing with her.[13]

There is little doubt that Jonathan was deeply impressed by Sarah's spirituality and her Christian maturity. Sarah's sweetness—her sweetness of mind and temper, her sweet singing, and the "exceeding sweet delight" that she had for God—especially appealed to Edwards, for whom the adjective *sweet* and its derivatives were frequently on his lips when he spoke of God and divine things.[14] It is not surprising that Jonathan does not mention in this paragraph what others frequently remarked on, namely, Sarah's physical beauty. Samuel Hopkins (1721–1803), who lived with the Edwardses while he was being informally tutored by Jonathan and later wrote an early memoir of his mentor, recalled that Sarah was "comely and beautiful."[15] For Jonathan, it was evidently and primarily the inner beauty of the soul that attracted him to Sarah.

In Her Own Words

An obscure magazine, *The Panoplist and Missionary Magazine United*, published a piece entitled "Relic of Mrs. Edwards," which contains a rare account of Sarah's early Christian experience that appears to be genuine.[16] According to the editor of this magazine, the paragraphs that follow were taken, "with a few verbal alterations, from a paper in the hand-writing of Mrs. Sarah Edwards" that was "dated Oct. 22, 1735."[17]

I have been this day looking over my grounds of hope, concerning my future state, and am not without hopes that my peace is made with God. About nine years ago, I was led to see my danger of eternal destruction; but I had a resolution given me to seek for mercy. I thought if I ever perished, it would be at the feet of the Redeemer. The words, *Though he slay me, yet will I put my trust in him,* often occurred to my mind.

Not long after this, the 44th of Isaiah, 4th, 5th, and 6th verses, were very heart-melting words to me. They seemed to be God's call to me, and I hope I was enabled by faith to hear and obey it. The next Sabbath I was led to prize nearness to Christ as the creature's greatest happiness. My soul thirsted for him, so that death seemed nothing to me, that I might be with him; for he was altogether lovely. This frame of mind continued for some time.

The winter after, I had a greater sense of my own vileness than ever. I could truly say, *I abhorred myself, and repented in dust and ashes.* It was not on account of the evil which sin would bring upon me; but because it dishonored God. This view of sin had a great tendency to humble me, and to incline me to go to God for pardon. I had great confidence in my love to Christ; and was not afraid to appeal to him, as Peter did, and say, *Lord, thou knowest all things; thou knowest that I love thee.* I loved Christ for what he was in himself; I loved him in all his offices; I saw my absolute need of him in all his offices; and I thought I was as willing to be ruled by his laws, as to be saved by his merits. I found a disposition to go to God as to a father. A soul-emptying and God-exalting way of being saved, was what I greatly delighted in. The thoughts of my heart were, *What have I that I have not received?* and, *Who hath made me to differ?* I felt great love to the people of God; even if they were persons whom I before disliked; yet then I felt an endearing affection towards them, and a delight in their company.

For half a year after, I had very little fear of death. Christ, I knew, had conquered death. During this time, I had such inward peace and rest of soul, in reflecting upon these things, as I cannot express. The vanity of the world was much in my thoughts. It seemed almost impossible, that I should ever be in the least uneasy at any thing I might meet with in the world; for all things were at the disposal of God. That was enough to cause me, with patience and humility, to bear whatever might befall me. I thought that Lam. iii, 39, *Wherefore doth a living man complain, a man for the punishment of his sins?* must command the silence of all, though they should meet with things ever so contrary to their minds.

In July 1727, I married and removed from New Haven to Northampton. For some time before I came here, it was almost all my request, that God would come with me. The prayer of Moses was much in my heart. And I hope God hath been with me here.

The fall after my arrival, I was exercised with fear that I was like the stony-ground hearers. I was afraid that, if tried with persecution, I should fall away. But God shewed me, that he could easily make me willing to die for his cause, if he called me to it; and that through Christ strengthening me, I could rejoice in the flames.

I have often had a spirit to rejoice in God as the portion of my soul, and my earnest desire has been, that I might come near to him even to his seat; and I esteemed a day in his courts better than a thousand elsewhere. I rejoiced that God reigns.

During a time of great affliction, I could often say, *Whom have I in heaven but thee? And there is none on earth that I desire beside thee. My soul thirsteth for God, for the living God. When shall I come and appear before God?*

I often said in my heart, there is joy in believing. I earnestly desired to imitate the example of Christ, in patience, and humility, and self-denial.

In this text Sarah engages in a typical Puritan-like reflection on the reasons she has to believe that she is truly a child of God. The fact that ultimately she delighted in a salvation that was "soul-emptying and God-exalting" was critical to her peace of mind regarding the authenticity of her conversion.

After her marriage to Jonathan in 1727 Sarah would have been kept extremely busy with domestic concerns, for the couple had eleven children between 1728 and 1750. While Jonathan certainly played a significant role as spiritual mentor to his children,[18] much of the raising of the children fell to Sarah. Understandably the pressure of these parental duties and all the other chores of running a busy household seems to have weighed heavily on Sarah. To cope Sarah gave herself and all that she was unreservedly to God on at least a couple of distinct occasions in 1739 and 1740.[19]

These self-dedications—in the Puritan tradition of making a personal covenant with God—were to be the foundation of some extraordinary experiences in late January and early February 1742. Jonathan was away from Northampton for much of this time on a two-week preaching tour that involved at least eight meetings in Massachusetts and Connecticut. While he was away, other ministers—among whom the most notable was Samuel Buell (d. 1798), who eventually settled at East Hampton, Long Island, and whose ordination sermon Edwards preached in 1746—filled the pulpit at Northampton.[20] Sarah was disturbed by a number of things at the time, in particular, a remark that her husband had said just before he had left on his preaching tour that he believed Sarah "had failed in some measure in point of prudence, in some conversation I had with Mr. [Chester] Williams," the minister in nearby Hadley and a distant cousin. Sarah was distressed that she did not "have the good opinion of my husband." [21] Other stresses—for example, finances and jealousy with regard to God's blessing upon the ministry of others in Northampton such as Buell and Williams—have led some to suggest that Sarah's experiences were part and parcel of a nervous breakdown. Elisabeth Dodds, for instance, describes Sarah becoming "grotesque—jabbering, hallucinating, and idiotically fainting."[22] Edwards was surely right to see his wife's experiences as a genuine encounter with the triune

God and the stresses in her life as God's means to bring her to the point of absolute submission to his sweet sovereignty.[23]

"Benign, Meek, Beneficent, Beatifical, Glorious Distraction"

When Edwards returned from his preaching trip, he asked Sarah to write down an account of her experiences. Edwards carefully edited Sarah's account so as to remove any indication of the identity and gender of the author and changed each personal pronoun to "the person," and he then inserted his edited version into *Some Thoughts*.

Sarah was given, we read,

> such views of the glory of the divine perfections, and Christ's excellencies, that the soul in the meantime has been as it were perfectly overwhelmed, and swallowed up with light and love and a sweet solace, rest and joy of soul, that was altogether unspeakable; and more than once continuing for five or six hours together, without any interruption, in that clear and lively view or sense of the infinite beauty and amiableness of Christ's person, and the heavenly sweetness of his transcendent love; so that (to use the person's own expressions) the soul remained in a kind of heavenly Elysium, and did as it were swim in the rays of Christ's love, like a little mote swimming in the beams of the sun, or beams of his light that come in at a window; and the heart was swallowed up in a kind of glow of Christ's love, coming down from Christ's heart in heaven, as a constant stream of sweet light, at the same time the soul all flowing out in love to him; so that there seemed to be a constant flowing and reflowing from heart to heart.[24]

On the other hand, there were times that Sarah had "a deep and lively sense" of her "own exceeding littleness and vileness."[25] She had

> an extraordinary sense of the awful majesty and greatness of God, . . . a sense of the holiness of God, as of a flame infinitely

pure and bright, . . . a sense of the piercing all-seeing eye of God, . . . and an extraordinary view of the infinite terribleness of the wrath of God, . . . together with a sense of the ineffable misery of sinners who are exposed to this wrath, that has been overbearing: sometimes the exceeding pollution of the person's own heart, as a sink of all manner of abomination, and a nest of vipers, and the dreadfulness of an eternal hell of God's wrath, opened to view both together.[26]

But foundational to all these profound experiences was

a sweet rejoicing of soul at the thoughts of God being infinitely and unchangeably happy, and an exulting gladness of heart that God is self-sufficient, and infinitely above all dependence, and reigns over all, and does his will with absolute and un-controllable power and sovereignty . . . [and the person's] soul often entertained, with unspeakable delight . . . the thoughts of heaven, as a world of love, where love shall be the saints' eternal food, and they shall dwell in the light of love, and swim in an ocean of love, and where the very air and breath will be nothing but love; love to the people of God, or God's true saints, as such that have the image of Christ, and as those who will in a very little time shine in his perfect image, that has been attended with that endearment and oneness of heart, and that sweetness and ravishment of soul, that has been alto-gether inexpressible.[27]

Now, accompanying these various experiences were certain unusual bodily phenomena, over twenty of them by one reckon-ing.[28] These "views of divine things," we are told, often deprived her body of "all ability to stand or speak."[29] When Sarah was given an "extraordinary sense of the awful majesty and greatness of God," she lost all bodily strength.[30] Another time, it was the "overwhelming sense of the glory of the work of redemption, and the way of salvation by Jesus Christ" which caused her body to faint.[31] On yet another occasion, "a sense of the glory of the Holy

Spirit, as the great Comforter," was such "as to overwhelm both soul and body."[32] On occasion, she was so taken with the joy of knowing such an awesome God that she had "to leap with all the might, with joy and mighty exultation of soul."[33]

Edwards, though, was at pains to point out that Sarah's joy was never attended "with the least appearance of any laughter or lightness of countenance." On the contrary, it led to "a new engagedness of heart to live to God's honor, and watch and fight against sin."[34] This view of the Christian life as a warfare against sin is typically Puritan. Nor were her experiences attended with any leanings toward sinless perfection, which Edwards notes as being the "the notion of the Wesleys and their followers, and some other high pretenders to spirituality in these days."[35] This reference to the Wesleyan doctrine of Christian perfection, which we looked at in the previous chapter, appears to be the only public reference of Edwards to the Wesley brothers.

Sarah's experiences did not involve "any enthusiastic [i.e., fanatical] disposition to follow impulses, or any supposed prophetical revelations."[36] Edwards was ever insistent that the Spirit of God always leads those whom he indwells to view the Scriptures as "the great and standing rule for the direction of his church in all religious matters, and all concerns of their souls, in all ages."[37] "Enthusiasts" or fanatics, on the other hand, regularly "depreciate this written rule, and set up the light within or some other rule above it."[38] In other words, Sarah's experiences were proven genuine by her refusal to look for God in any other place but his divine Word.

Moreover, what helped Edwards come to a decision about the divine source of these experiences were their fruit in daily life. Sarah did not feel that her experiences elevated her above others. On the contrary, she had

a peculiar sensible aversion to judging others that were professing Christians of good standing in the visible church, that they were not converted, or with respect to their degrees of grace; or at all intermeddling with that matter, so much as to determine against and condemn others in the thought of the heart; it appearing hateful, as not agreeing with that lamb-like humility, meekness, gentleness, and charity, which the soul then, above other times, saw the beauty of, and felt a disposition to.[39]

Humility and meekness were something that Edwards regularly emphasized as a sure mark of being filled with the Spirit. Edwards also noted that his wife had a deepened sense of her need to help the poor.[40] Moreover, as he watched his wife engaged in her daily responsibilities in their home, he saw a person who was now "eating for God, and working for God, and sleeping for God, and bearing pain and trouble for God, and doing all as the service of love, and so doing it with a continual, uninterrupted cheerfulness, peace and joy."[41] There was not the slightest desire to neglect "the necessary business" of her calling as a wife and mother. "Worldly business has been attended with great alacrity, as part of the service of God." Sarah told her husband that when she did her work thus, it was "as good as prayer."[42]

Little wonder then that Edwards can burst out, at the conclusion of his edited account of Sarah's experience:

> Now if such things are enthusiasm, and the fruits of a distempered brain, let my brain be evermore possessed of that happy distemper! If this be distraction, I pray God that the world of mankind may be all seized with this benign, meek, beneficent, beatifical, glorious distraction![43]

But without the presence of this God-centeredness, the physical manifestations would have been of no value and would actually have been detrimental to genuine piety. Sarah thus anonymously became a model of what true revival personally looks like.[44]

Divine Benevolence

There is one other statement in this section of *Some Thoughts* of which note needs to be taken. Part of Sarah's experience, Edwards wrote, was

> an universal benevolence to mankind, with a longing as it were to embrace the whole world in the arms of pity and love; ideas of suffering from enemies the utmost conceivable rage and cruelty, with a disposition felt to fervent love and pity in such a case, so far as it could be realized in thought; fainting with pity to the world that lies in ignorance and wickedness; sometimes a disposition was felt to a life given up to mourning alone in a wilderness over a lost and miserable world; compassion towards them being often to that degree, that would allow of no support or rest, but in going to God, and pouring out the soul in prayer for them; earnest desires that the work of God; that is now in the land, may be carried on, and that with greater purity, and freedom from all bitter zeal, censoriousness, spiritual pride, hot disputes, etc.
>
> A vehement and constant desire for the setting up of Christ's kingdom through the earth, as a kingdom of holiness, purity, love, peace, and happiness to mankind . . .[45]

What Sarah displayed here was, in her husband's mind, true divine love, which he would later define in *The Nature of True Virtue* (1755, published 1765) as "love of benevolence," which is that "affection or propensity of heart to any being, which causes it to incline it to its well-being, or disposes it to desire and take pleasure in its happiness."[46] This sort of love does not require any beauty in its object. On the other hand, love that did require its object to be beautiful was what Edwards called "love of complacence."[47] Clearly God's love for sinners is of the first kind. And what thrilled Edwards about his wife's experiences was that this sort of love, this love of benevolence that loves regardless of the beauty of the object, attended them. In the words of James Wm. McClendon, what "God had given her was love understood as cordial consent, her capacity to say yes to God and to all that was God's."[48]

And surely it was this sort of love that Edwards was referring to on his deathbed when he spoke of "the uncommon union," which had so long subsisted between himself and his wife, which "has been of such a nature, as I trust is spiritual, and therefore will continue forever."[49] Their benevolent love for God and his world—truly uncommon in this selfish, sinful world—had bonded them together during their married life. It was a "spiritual" love. As McClendon well puts it, they were "two who have breathed together the breath of the same Spirit."[50] And as such, it was eternal for it had joined them to the triune God.

5

Anne Steele and Her Hymns

"The Tuneful Tongue That Sung . . .
Her Great Redeemer's Praise"[1]

By common acknowledgment all the great hymn writers of the eighteenth century were men—Isaac Watts (1674–1748), Charles Wesley (1707–1788), William Cowper (1731–1800), and John Newton (1725–1807), for example—all, that is, except one, Anne Steele (1717–1778), who has been well described as "the Baptist equivalent of Isaac Watts."[2] Born into a leading Calvinistic Baptist family on the south of England, her hymns were written, in the first place, as vehicles of personal devotion. But her father, William Steele, the pastor of the Baptist Chapel at Broughton, Hampshire, liked them so much that he began to have them sung during worship in their church. In time, some of her hymns were included in a Baptist hymnal, and two years after her death—she died in 1778—Caleb Evans (1737–1791), a tutor at the Bristol Baptist Academy at the time, and John Ash (1724–1779), the Baptist pastor of Pershore, Worcestershire, published a three-volume set of her hymns and poems. A few of her hymns, such as "Father of mercies, in thy Word," are still in use today.

Anne's Church and Anne's Family in Broughton

Broughton is a small, peaceful village in the south of England, exactly midway between the two cathedral towns of Salisbury and Winchester. The Steeles were one of the more prosperous families in the community—Anne's father, William, the pastor of the church, and her brother, also William, were heavily involved in the timber trade, selling to the British Navy lumber that would serve as masts for their ships and that involved hundreds, even thousands, of pounds. For quite a while, the Steeles were the leading family in the Calvinistic Baptist Chapel in Broughton, which was one of the oldest in the country.

One hundred and eleven Christians had first met together in 1653 to found a Baptist church in Porton, Wiltshire, a few miles north of Salisbury.[3] By 1710 it had relocated to Broughton, a few miles to the east on the River Wallop. Nine were baptized at the first meeting. The church survived the vicious years of persecution from 1660 to 1688. In 1699, ten years after the Act of Toleration was passed, which brought religious freedom for Nonconformists outside of the Church of England, Henry Steele (1655–1739) became pastor. He had already been a member for nineteen years and had been engaged in itinerant preaching. He remained the pastor for the next forty years until 1739. He refused to take any financial support from the church, as he had made a fortune in contracting for timber—English oak—for the Royal Navy. Much of the profit was then invested in farmland.[4] There is a story that Henry Steele was such a popular preacher that the local Church of England minister complained to the bishop that Steele was taking away his congregation, only to receive the unsympathetic reply that if he preached as well as Steele, his congregation would return to him.[5]

Henry had no son, so his nephew William (Anne's father) assisted him in his business and also in the preaching. As it turned out, William ended up taking over both Henry's business and the pastorate in 1739. His family home was an elegant and spacious dwelling called "Grandfathers," which can be still seen today in the village. William's first wife was Anne Froude, the daughter of the Baptist minister Edward Froude, who had signed the Second London Confession of Faith in 1689. Here at Grandfathers the couple rejoiced at the birth of a son and a daughter, named after themselves, William (b. 1714) and Anne. Sadly, when another baby arrived in 1720, both mother and infant died. William was thus left alone to take care of five-year-old William and three-year-old Anne.

Three years later, in 1723, he remarried—another Anne, who followed the Puritan tradition of keeping a diary. The volumes with her entries for the years 1731–1735, 1748–1749, and 1753–1760 have survived. These were the years that her stepdaughter, Anne, was thirteen to eighteen, thirty-one to thirty-two, and thirty-six to forty-three.[6] These journal entries give valuable evidence about the life of Anne Steele. They also show that her stepmother, Anne Cater Steele, was a woman of deep piety. She took her responsibility for her stepchildren William and Anne (nicknamed Nany or Nanny) very seriously indeed. Her diary, for example, records times of "sweet" or "delightful" conversation about spiritual things with young Anne, her stepdaughter.

Life for the Steele children revolved around the regular meetings of the Baptist church. The research of Baptist historian Karen Smith has provided a cameo of what life and worship were like for Calvinistic Baptists at this time.[7] While William and Anne were small, they were accustomed to hearing their great-uncle Henry preach. Services on Sunday mornings and afternoons were simple in order: extemporary prayers offered by the minister, metrical psalms and hymns "lined out" by one of the congregation, and the sermon. Sometimes there were meetings for informal discussion on Sunday evenings, and there was at least one mid-week prayer meeting.

Baptisms were conducted in the baptistery, which had been constructed by 1727 (the person who filled it received payment of one shilling). It was quite unusual at this time for a church to have an indoor baptistery. Normally, baptism was done outside in a river, lake, or pond. Baptismal candidates wore special clothes: a long robe for the men and a plain, white, long dress for the women. The Lord's Supper was celebrated once a month, preceded by serious preparation, both corporate and individual. The table was "closed," that is, only baptized believers in membership of that church or another recognized fellowship could participate. New members would be welcomed into the fellowship at the Lord's Supper following their baptism. Membership was a serious commitment: attendance at the meetings was expected but also adherence to the covenant, which committed members to prayer for one another and mutual support. Nonattendance or obvious violation of biblical standards or the covenant was punished at first with suspension from the Lord's Supper and ultimately with excommunication. Discipline was carried out, and occasionally there were serious cases, as in 1732, the year of Anne's baptism as a believer, when a certain Betty Jones left her husband and ran off with the pastor of another Baptist congregation.

Membership at Broughton Baptist Church stood at around fifty-one when Anne was fourteen, in 1731. The next year, she and her brother William both gave their testimony to the church meeting and were baptized, along with nine others. It was customary in the eighteenth century for applicants for baptism and church membership to give an extemporary verbal account of their conversion. Baptists, as we have seen, cherished the "gathered church" principle, namely, only truly converted people were to be considered as prospective members. While they looked anxiously for "signs" of conversion in their young children, who often professed faith, it was common to wait at least until mid-teens before young people "gave in their experience." Note, this was one of the few times that females could speak in the church meeting. Some people found the "giving in of their testimony" an unnerving experience, and many churches softened the demand during the following century, allowing them to submit a written testimony or else relying on a membership interview with at least two senior members or officers.

As we have noted, in 1739, when Anne was twenty-two, her great-uncle Henry died. He had been pastor for forty years. Her father, William, had been assisting him and preaching regularly for many years, and at this time he took over the pastorate. The church was enjoying a time of growth—this in contrast to the overall decline of the denomination in many areas of the country. Just eight years later, in 1745, the membership peaked at ninety-one. There had been many baptisms (thirty-seven in the period from 1730–1739), but after 1745 things began to decline, and in the following decade there were only four baptisms recorded. Things improved after that, and from 1759–1768 there were twelve new members, all but one coming in through confession of faith and baptism.

Anne's father William was a successful businessman, and he continued to support himself through the timber trade. But he was also a devoted pastor. His second wife threw herself into the life of the church, and his children were also keen members. Anne's sensitivity to the needs of public worship inspired her to write hymns on the whole range of themes appropriate to different occasions and to fit the range of topics covered in the preaching ministry.

Anne's Early Years

Educational opportunities at home were deemed to be limited, and thus, as was common among more prosperous families, the Steele children were sent to boarding school.[8] There was a dissenting academy for training ministers at nearby Trowbridge, and Anne was sent to a boarding school for girls that was probably linked to this academy. It is not known how long Anne stayed at this school. Anne also went to a very wealthy boarding school in Salisbury when she was sixteen.

We have no firm knowledge of the content of Anne's formal education, but just as important was the ongoing education provided by correspondence with her family's circle of friends and evenings at home when friends visited. Among her correspondents were a number of Baptist ministers: John Lavington (1690–1759) from the Exeter Baptist Church; Philip Furneaux (1726–1783) from London; James Fanch (1704–1767) from Romsey; Caleb Evans of Bristol; and John Ash of Pershore, Worcestershire.[9] Furneaux helped get her work published in 1760, and Evans and Ash collaborated on a further edition of her poems after her death.

When family and friends visited, a typical social evening involved conversation on a wide variety of topics, and sometimes the reading of poetry and other literature. We know of one occasion when the great literary evangelical Hannah More (1745–1833) visited Anne in Broughton.[10] Anne also traveled widely, visiting relatives in Hampshire, Wiltshire, and Somerset.[11] Anne also had access to her father's "extensive library of Puritan and eighteenth century theology," in which she appears to have been well read.[12]

When Anne was fourteen, there is the first of many references in the diary of Anne Steele's stepmother to "the ague," which a modern doctor has argued convincingly was probably recurring malaria. Anne suffered from this throughout her life, the major consequences of which would have been anemia, weakness, and susceptibility to other infections. It also issued in high fevers and left Anne vulnerable to consumption.[13]

Malaria was common in England at the time and was especially associated with marshy, low-lying areas, and Anne's home, "Grandfathers," was right near some water meadows by the River Wallop. Anne never seems to have enjoyed any sustained periods of good health, and all too often she was in great pain. Effective painkillers were unknown in Anne's day, and the means used by doctors only exacerbated the suffering. Common remedies were bleeding (by knife or leech); blistering (agonizingly painful, supposed to draw out bad bodily fluids); and inducing vomiting. All of this was a relic of the old belief that sickness was the effect of an imbalance of "humours" or bodily fluids.

From the age of fourteen onward, Anne's health was a constant worry to her stepmother, and there are many anguished references to this in her stepmother's diary. Anne seems to have suffered from terrible stomach pain (probably a peptic ulcer), and from agonizing toothache (common enough in a century when dental hygiene was primitive and treatment barbaric).[14] Her stepmother was told that Anne probably had consumption, and she often confided in her diary that Anne's death was imminent. When Anne was eighteen, she was thrown from a horse and hurt her hip. But, as there is no further mention of this, it certainly did not leave her a lifelong invalid as some biographers of Anne have inferred.[15]

When Anne was thirty-four her health was so bad that she went to Bath with her sister for the months of May and June in order to take the waters. The visit was not especially happy, as Anne was too ill much of the time to bathe or even to drink the waters. She was ill for much of her thirty-seventh year. When she was forty there were the first indications of a nervous disorder (which fits with the prognosis of malaria), and at the age of forty-three the first indications of shortness of breath. From then until she was fifty-four there were fluctuating periods of good and bad health, but from the age of fifty-four until her death six years later she was effectively housebound. Anne's own experience of suffering, and her conscious acceptance of it from the hand of God, meant that her poems and hymns on this theme struck a real chord with other sufferers.

Singleness: A Conscious Choice

By the time Anne was twenty she may have commenced a courtship with a young man called Mr. Elcomb, who subsequently drowned in a bathing accident. Elcomb had gone to the River Wallop to wash, went out of his depth, and was swept away by the current.[16] The Baptist historian Joseph Ivimey in 1830 romantically wrote that this tragedy happened the day before the wedding of Anne and Elcomb. It then became popular to think that Anne's nerves never recovered. But there is no evidence either in Anne's subsequent writings or in the diaries of her stepmother to indicate that she suffered from a perpetually broken heart.[17]

We do know that when Anne was twenty-five, she received a proposal of marriage from the minister of the Particular Baptist Chapel at Bourton-on-the-Water, Benjamin Beddome (1717–1795). He too was twenty-five, and he poured out his heart in a passionate proposal, even likening his seeing her to Adam's first sight of Eve in John Milton's *Paradise Lost*.[18] We have no record of Anne's reply. It seems that Beddome's eloquence failed to persuade her. Beddome evidently recovered sufficiently from his disappointment to marry Elizabeth Bothwell at a later date.

Anne received another proposal of marriage later in life, but she made a conscious choice to remain single. In a letter she wrote to her stepsister after refusing one of these proposals—possibly that of Beddome, though possibly not—she said that the suitor had offered his hand to help over the stile, that is, get married. But when she looked over into the meadow of marriage, she writes, "I looked over and saw no flowers, but observed a great many thorns, and I suppose there are more hid under the leaves, but as there is not verdure enough to cover half of 'em it must be near winter, as I think it generally happens when I look into the said Meadow."[19]

Anne's Hymns

So Anne remained single. But her singleness gave her the time to devote herself to poetry and hymn writing, a gift with which the Lord had richly blessed her. About ten years before her death, sixty-two of her hymns were published in the Baptist hymnal entitled *A Collection of Hymns Adapted to Public Worship* (1769), better known as the "Bristol Collection," produced for the Calvinistic Baptists by two pastors: Caleb Evans and John Ash. This hymnal gave her hymns a wide circulation throughout Baptist circles,[20] and in time her hymns became as well known in Baptist circles as those of Isaac Watts.

Anne provided hymns on the whole range of topics useful in public worship: baptism, the Lord's Supper, the three persons of the Trinity, the free offer of the gospel. But Anne wrote on many other themes, such as creation, the exaltation of Christ, assurance, national hymns, funeral hymns, approaching death, and victory over death. Many of her hymns focus on the transience of this life and God the only true good.

When Anne died in 1778, she was mourned by her brother, his second wife, her nieces and nephews, the church circle, and many friends. But she was as yet unknown to the wider Christian public, as her poems and hymns had appeared under her pen name Theodosia. This anonymity was just what she had wanted during her lifetime. Two years after her death, her identity became public knowledge when Caleb Evans republished the poems and hymns.

The Free Offer of the Gospel

In chapter 3, we noted that the Particular or Calvinistic Baptists in England for a good part of the eighteenth century were in decline. One of the very few of Anne's hymns that is still sung today reveals the way in which the wide circulation of her hymns played a part in revitalizing the Calvinistic Baptist cause throughout England. The hymn was originally entitled "The Savior's Invitation" and was based on Jesus's words in John 7:37, "If any man thirst, let him come unto me, and drink" (KJV).

> The Saviour calls—let every Ear
> Attend the heavenly Sound;
> Ye doubting Souls, dismiss your Fear,
> Hope smiles reviving round.
>
> For every thirsty, longing Heart,
> Here Streams of Bounty flow,
> And Life, and Health, and Bliss impart,

To banish mortal Woe.

Here, Springs of sacred Pleasure rise
To ease your every Pain,
(Immortal Fountain! full Supplies!)
Nor shall you thirst in vain.

Ye Sinners come, 'tis Mercy's Voice,
The gracious Call obey;
Mercy invites to heavenly Joys,—
And can you yet delay?

Dear Savior, draw reluctant Hearts,
To Thee let Sinners fly;
And take the Bliss Thy Love imparts,
And drink, and never die.[21]

Based on Jesus's open invitation to sinners to come to him and drink, that is, find eternal life, Steele urges "every Ear" to "attend" to Christ's heavenly invitation. He calls all who are "thirsty" and "longing" to come to him, where they will find "Life, and Health, and Bliss"; in sum, "Springs of sacred Pleasure" that will ease every woe. This invitation is a command—"the gracious Call obey"—and a free offer—"can you yet delay?"[22] But Steele is also aware that the "thirsty, longing Heart" is not sufficient in itself to come to Christ. In the final analysis it is a "reluctant Heart," filled with doubt and fear. Hence, she prays, "Dear Savior, draw reluctant hearts." And this is a prayer that can be prayed with confidence, for the Savior to whom she speaks is an "Immortal Fountain," Mercy incarnate who loves sinners and delights in bestowing on them "heavenly Joys." As Baptist men and women of England sang such hymns, God was preparing them for revival.

Similarly, in her hymn "To our Redeemer's glorious name," after the congregation has sung:

Jesus, who left His throne on high,
Left the bright realms of bliss,

And came on earth to bleed and die—
Was ever love like this?

Anne offers this prayer for all who are within the sound of the singers and the preacher—believers and unbelievers:

> Dear Lord, while we adoring pay
> Our humble thanks to Thee,
> May every heart with rapture say,
> The Savior died for me.
>
> O may the sweet, the blissful theme
> Fill every heart and tongue,
> Till strangers love Thy charming Name,
> And join the sacred song.[23]

The emphasis on "every heart and tongue and "strangers" bespeaks an evangelistic passion to see the gospel have a profound impact on her society and world.

Word-Centered and Christ-Centered

Among the few of Anne's hymns that still retain currency is "Father of mercies, in thy word," which reveals Anne's delight in the Scriptures, typical of the piety of her Baptist community:

> Father of mercies, in thy word
> What endless glory shines!
> For ever be thy name adored
> For these celestial lines.
>
> . . . O may these heavenly pages be
> My ever dear delight,
> And still new beauties may I see,
> And still increasing light.
>
> Divine instructor, gracious Lord,
> Be thou for ever near;

Teach me to love thy sacred word,
And view my Saviour here.[24]

Note that the supreme value of the Scriptures for Anne is that in them she finds and sees her Savior, the Lord Jesus. As she confesses in another hymn, "Thou lovely source of true delight":

Thou lovely source of true delight
Whom I unseen adore
Unveil Thy beauties to my sight
That I might love Thee more.

Thy glory o'er creation shines
But in Thy sacred Word
I read in fairer, brighter lines
My bleeding, dying Lord.[25]

The revelation of the beauty of Christ was, for Anne, deeply intertwined with the experience of reading and hearing: it was in the "fairer, brighter lines" of Holy Scripture that she saw her Lord.

6

Esther Edwards Burr
on Friendship

"One of the Best Helps to Keep
Up Religion in the Soul"

Our culture is not one that provides great encouragement for the nurture and development of deep, long-lasting, satisfying friendships. Such friendships take time and sacrifice, and early twenty-first-century Western culture is a busy, busy world that, as a rule, is far more interested in receiving and possessing than sacrificing and giving.[1] What is especially disturbing about this fact is that Western Christianity is little different from its culture. The English Anglican writer C. S. Lewis (1898–1963) wrote an ingenious little book entitled *The Screwtape Letters*, a remarkable commentary on spiritual warfare from the point of view of our Enemy. In it there is one letter from the senior devil, Screwtape, to his nephew Wormwood in which Screwtape rejoices over the fact that "in modern Christian writings" there is to be found "few of the old warnings about worldly vanities, the choice of friends, and the value of time."[2] Now, whether or not Lewis is right with regard to a scarcity of Christian literature about "worldly vanities" and "the value of time" in the modern world, he is undoubtedly correct when it comes to the topic of friendship.

Thinking about Friendship

How different in this respect is our world from that of the ancients, both pagan and Christian. In the ancient world friendship was deemed to be of such vital importance that the pagan philosopher Plato (c. 428/427–348/347 BC) devoted an entire book, the *Lysis*, as well as substantial portions of two other books, the *Phaedrus* and the *Symposium*, to a treatment of its nature. Aristotle (384–322 BC), the other leading thinker of the classical Greek period, also considered the topic of friendship significant enough to have a discussion of it occupy two of the ten books of the *Nicomachean Ethics*, his major work on ethical issues. For the ancient Greeks—and this is true also of the Romans—friendship formed one of the highest ideals of human life.

While we do not find such extended discussions of the concept of friendship in the Scriptures, we do come across reflections on friendship such as Ecclesiastes 4:7–12 and marvelous illustrations of what friendship should be like, for example, Ruth and Naomi, or David and Jonathan. In that Old Testament compendium of wisdom, Proverbs, there are also nuggets of advice about having friends and keeping them. These texts leave the impression that the world of the Bible regards friendship as a very important part of life.

Now, the Bible uses two images in its representation of friendship.[3] The first is the knitting together of souls. Deuteronomy provides the earliest mention in this regard of a "friend who is as your own soul" (Deut. 13:6), that is, one who is knit together with your soul or one who is a companion of one's innermost thoughts and feelings. It is well illustrated by Jonathan and David's friendship, as depicted in 1 Samuel 18:1, 3–4, where the same phrase is used as in Deuteronomy 13. Here we see ideas of strong emotional attachment and loyalty.[4] In fact, "friend" naturally became another name for believers or brothers in the Lord (3 John 15). The privileges and responsibilities of a biblical soul mate, then, involve intimacy, loyalty, and a strong emotional attachment.

The second image that the Bible uses to represent friendship is the face-to-face encounter. This is the image used for Moses's relationship to God: in the tabernacle God spoke to Moses "face to face, as a man speaks to his friend" (Ex. 33:11; see also Num. 12:8). The face-to-face image implies a conversation, a sharing of confidences and consequently a meeting of minds, goals, and direction.[5] One of the benefits of face-to-face encounters between friends is the heightened insight that such encounters produce. A proverb that highlights this idea is the famous one in Proverbs 27:17: "Iron sharpens iron, and one man sharpens another."

There are a number of fabulous illustrations of this sort of biblical friendship in the history of the church. This chapter looks at that of Esther Edwards Burr (1732–1758) and Sarah Prince (1728–1771).[6]

Esther's Early Years

Esther Edwards Burr was born in Northampton, Massachusetts, on February 13, 1732, the third child of Jonathan and Sarah Edwards, whom we looked at in chapter 4. Of Esther's early years, we know very little. Samuel Hopkins, who wrote the first biography of her father, Jonathan Edwards, and who lived in their home for over a year, remembered her as having "a lively, sprightly imagination, a quick and penetrating thought."[7]

Her childhood years coincided with the years of the Great Awakening. She was eight when the Great Awakening began, and she heard George Whitefield preach to her father's congregation in October of that year; she was ten when it ended in 1742. All of this would have made a deep impression on her.[8] The revival would no doubt have reinforced in her mind that genuine Christianity was a religion of the heart and that "the only true religion was indeed heartfelt, nothing short of a total and joyous submission to the will of God."[9] She herself made a profession of faith before the church when she was "about fifteen," though her conversion is to be dated earlier—possibly when Whitefield preached to the Northampton congregation.[10]

Marriage and a Move to Newark

On June 29, 1752, at the age of twenty, Esther married Aaron Burr Sr. (1715–1757), a minister whose evangelical cast of mind was much like her own and who was deeply respected by her father.[11] Aaron was the pastor of the Presbyterian church in Newark, New Jersey, and the second president of the newly formed College of New Jersey there (later to be called Princeton when it moved to the town of that name during Burr's presidency). He was considerably older than Esther—seventeen years to be exact—which occasioned some gossip. One of the students at the College, Joseph Shippen, reckoned Esther a "great beauty" when he saw her, but far "too young for the president."[12] Later, though, Shippen was positively glowing in his appreciation of the Burrs' marriage, and he called Esther a woman of "very good sense, of a genteel & virtuous education, amiable in her person, of great affability & agreeableness in conversation & a very excellent economist."[13]

Aaron Burr had last seen Esther when she was fourteen, but it took only a few days of courtship for Esther to agree to marry Aaron. The apparent suddenness of her decision may well have had something to do with the financial strains on the Edwards family at the time, since Jonathan Edwards had been dismissed from the Northampton pastorate in 1750 two years earlier.[14] But there is every evidence that she deeply loved Aaron. As she said in her *Journal*, "Do you think I would change my *good Mr Burr* for any person, or thing, or all things on the Erth? *No sure!* Not for a Million such Worlds as this that had *no Mr Burr in it.*"[15]

Esther's move to Newark meant that she was some 150 miles away from her parents and family in Stockbridge, Massachusetts, a considerable distance to travel in that period of time. Moreover, New Jersey was quite different from either Massachusetts or Connecticut. While not as developed, it was far more cosmopolitan, which occasionally made Esther homesick for her roots in New England.[16] All this was exacerbated by the fact that her husband, as president of the college, was frequently away preaching and raising funds. Esther felt sufficiently "isolated" and hungry for the fellowship of "young women with spiritual and intellectual interests similar to her own"[17] to covenant with a close Boston friend, Sarah Prince—the daughter of Thomas Prince (1687–1758), pastor of Boston's Old South Church and a close friend of Edwards—to maintain their friendship by writing journals for one another. Esther tried to include an entry every day, but some days, especially Saturdays, she was hard-pressed to do so as the following entries indicate:

> June 5, 1756:
> All in the hurries with a great Ironing so cant get time to say any thing but that I think of you if I dont talk to you.

> June 12, 1756:
> Saturday all in the hurries—I hate these hurries of a Saturday. I would never have it so if I could help it.

> August 7, 1756:
> Saturday, Busy, Busy—*hurry, Fly—Run*.[18]

Esther had been in Newark about a year and a half when Sarah Prince traveled south from Boston in the autumn of 1753 to spend a number of months with her. Esther was expecting her first child during the time of Sarah's visit, and Sarah stayed up to the time of Esther's confinement. The naming of the first child, Sally (short for Sarah), seems to have been for the two most important women in her life, her mother and her best friend.[19]

An Edwardsean Piety

It should come as no surprise that Esther's piety is quite Edwardsean. Her delight in her father as a spiritual mentor is well seen in a *Journal* entry for September 19, 1756, when she wrote during a visit to her parents in Stockbridge:

> Last eve I had some free discourse with My Father on the great things that concern my best intrest—I opend my diffeculties to him very freely and he as freely advised and directed. The conversation has removed some distressing doubts that discouraged me much in my Christian warfare—He gave me some excellent directions to be observed in secret that tend to keep the soul near to God, as well as others to be observed in a more publick way—what a mercy that I have such a Father! Such a Guide![20]

Like her father, she was committed to a God who had revealed himself in salvation and history as a God of mercy[21] and sovereignty[22]: "Mercyfull, Wise, Powerfull, Good God that he was from Eternity, and so will continue to Eternity—altho all things Change, yet our God is what he always was."[23] And like her father, she emphasized the necessity of "heart religion." As she wrote on June 14, 1755:

> That knowledge of God that does not produce a love to him and a desire to be like him is not a true knowledge—that knowledge of any things that produces *love* will also produce a desire to be like what we know and *Love*—that the fallen Angels know much of God is sertain, and that the more they know of him, the more they hate him is as sertain, and that because their hearts are filled with enmity to all good.[24]

Friendship: A Means of Grace

Now, one of the most important things that Esther prized in keeping her near to God was spiritual conversation with close friends such as Sarah Prince:

I should highly value (as you my dear do) such *charming friends* as you have about *you—friends* that one might unbosom their whole soul too. . . . I esteem *religious conversation* one of the best helps to keep up religion in the soul, excepting secret devotion, I don't know but the very best—Then what a lamentable thing that 'tis so neglected by Gods own children.[25]

Note the connection between friendship and what Esther calls "religious conversation." For the Christian, true friends are those with whom one can share the deepest things of one's life. They are people with whom one can be transparent and open. In Esther's words, they are people to whom one can "unbosom [one's] whole soul." And in the course of conversation about spiritual things the believer can find strength and encouragement for living the Christian life. In referring to spiritual conversation with friends as "one of the best helps to keep up religion in the soul," Esther obviously views it as a means of grace, one of the ways that God the Holy Spirit keeps Christians in fellowship with the Savior. As another New England Christian, Nathanael Emmons (1745–1840), a theologian who was mentored by close followers of Jonathan Edwards, put it in one of his favorite maxims: "A man is made by his friends."[26]

This is the way Esther put the same thought on another occasion where she stresses the importance of Christian friendship as a means for walking with God:

Nothing is more refreshing to the soul (except communication with God himself) than the company and society of a friend— One that has the spirit of, and relish for, true friendship—this is becoming [to] the rational soul—this is God-like.[27]

And Sarah was such a friend, as Esther's entries for October 11, 1754, and June 4, 1755, reveal:

It is a great comfort to me when my friends are absent from me that I have 'em some where in the World, and you my dear for *one*, not of the least, for I esteem you one of the best, and in some respects nerer than any Sister I have. I have not one Sister I can write so freely to as to you the Sister of my heart.[28]

Consider my friend how rare a thing tis to meet with such a friend as I have in my *Fidelia*—Who would not vallue and prize such a friend above gold, or honour, or any thing that the World can afford?[29]

Esther was convinced that such friendship was a gift from heaven. As she put it in two journal entries—the first from October 5, 1754, and the second from February 15, 1755:

Mrs Smith and I were talking . . . and determined that whatsoever had been spoken in Confidence whiles there was supposed to be a friendship aught to be kept secret. Altho the friendship was at an end, yet the obligation was as strong as ever, and Mrs Smith thinks stronger. . . . I look on the ties of Friendship as *sacred*, and I am of your mind, that it aught to be a matter of Solemn Prayer to God (where there is a friendship contracted) that it may be preserved.[30]

You will think I am not so very indifferent to everything in the world nither, but to tell the truth when I speak of the *world*, and the things that are in the *World*, I don't mean *friends*, for *friendship* does not belong to the *world*. *True friendship* is first inkindled by a spark from *Heaven*, and *heaven* will never suffer it to go out, but it will *burn* to all *Eternity*.[31]

A year later, on January 23, 1756, she stated again her conviction about the vital need for Christian friends:

Tis my dear a great mercy that we have any friends—What would this World be with out 'em—A person who looks upon himself to be friendless must of all Cretures be missarable in this life—Tis the Life of Life.[32]

Note the way that Esther prizes Christian friends. For her, they are one of this world's greatest sources of happiness. Why did

Esther put such a value upon friendship? Well, surely because she realized that Christian friends and conversation with them is vital for spiritual growth.

Esther Challenged by John Ewing

Esther's convictions regarding friendship as such a means of grace were challenged in April 12, 1757, when one of the college tutors, John Ewing (1732–1802), who would later be a professor of ethics at the College of Philadelphia and the pastor of First Presbyterian in Philadelphia, challenged her understanding of friendship:

> I have had a smart Combat with Mr Ewing about our sex—he is a man of good parts and Lerning but has mean thoughts of Women—he began the dispute in this Manner. Speaking of Miss Boudanot I said she was a sociable friendly creture. . . . But Mr Ewing says—*she and the Stocktons are full of talk about Friendship and society and such stuff—and made up a Mouth as if much disgusted*—I asked what he would have 'em talk about—whether he chose they should talk about fashions and dress—*he said things that they understood. He did not think women knew what Friendship was. They were hardly capable of anything so cool and rational as friendship*—(My Tongue, you know, hangs pretty loose, thoughts Crouded in—so I sputtered away for dear life.) You may Guss what a large field this speach opened for me—I retorted several severe things upon him before he had time to speak again. He Blushed and seemed confused . . . we carried on the dispute for an hour—I talked him quite silent. He got up and said your servant and went off— . . . One of the last things that he said was that he never in all his life knew or heard of a woman that had a little more lerning then [common?] but it made her proud to such a degree that she was disgusfull [to] all her acquaintance.[33]

Ewing probably never forgot this encounter with Edwards's formidable daughter.[34] Esther knew from personal experience of her rich friendship with Sarah Prince what true friendship is all about and that Ewing had no idea of what he was talking about.

Esther's final comment about Ewing's disdain for women who were educated tells us much not only about him but also about Esther. Jonathan Edwards, her father, like his father, Timothy Edwards (1669–1758), believed in the value of educating daughters. Edwards was the fifth of his parents' eleven children—ten girls and Jonathan! Edwards's sisters grew to be tall women, each of them over six feet tall, and those who knew them often spoke of Timothy Edwards's "sixty feet of daughters"![35] Quite unusual for a seventeenth-century man, Timothy Edwards encouraged them to develop intellectually as well as spiritually.[36] In addition to giving his daughters an education similar to that of Jonathan, Timothy sent all but one of his daughters to a finishing school in Boston. All told, this education produced strong, spiritually focused women who were not afraid to speak their minds. As Esther's encounter with Ewing reveals, Jonathan's tutelage of his daughters had produced equally strong women as his own sisters.

7

Ann Judson and the
Missionary Enterprise

"Truth Compelled Us"

Historian David S. Schaff, son of the famous historian Phillip Schaff, was surely right when he noted that the name of Ann Hasseltine Judson (1789–1826) "is one of the immortal names in missionary biography."[1] Francis Wayland (1796–1865), the major nineteenth-century biographer of Ann's husband, said after he spent time with her in 1822: "I do not remember ever to have met a more remarkable woman." With her husband Adoniram Judson (1788–1850) she was the first of a long line of American evangelical missionaries. In fact, her embrace, and that of her husband, in 1812 of Baptist principles is one of the key turning points in the history of the American Baptists: it marked this community's entry into the modern missionary movement, an event sealed two years later by the formation of the Triennial Convention, so called because it met every three years. Moreover, Ann's life story was repeated innumerable times in the nineteenth and twentieth centuries—almost every year between 1830 and 1856 there was a new edition of her biography, which prompted one author, Lydia Maria Child, to describe it as "a book . . . universally known."[2] Thus, she became, along with her husband and others such as William Carey (1761–1834) and Hudson Taylor (1832–1905), a key source of inspiration for the modern missionary movement. In what follows, her life is sketched through a number of select letters, which detail her decision to become a missionary with her husband Adoniram, her becoming a Baptist, and, finally, her key work in the mission to Burma with her husband.

"I Feared to Displease God"

Born just before Christmas, 1789, in Bradford, Massachusetts, Ann Hasseltine was converted in a revival in her hometown in 1806, when she was a teenager. The revival was part of the larger movement known as the Second Great Awakening. In a diary she kept at the time, she mentioned that her

> chief happiness now consisted in contemplating the moral perfections of the glorious God. I longed to have all intelligent creatures love him. . . . Sin, in myself and others, appeared as that abominable thing, which a holy God hates,—and I earnestly strove to avoid sinning, not merely because I was afraid of hell, but because I feared to displease God, and grieve his Holy Spirit.[3]

Four years later, on June 28, 1810, Adoniram Judson, her future husband, came for lunch at her parents' home with three other students, all Congregationalists and all of whom had offered themselves to serve as missionaries with their body of churches under the auspices of what was called the American Board of Commissioners for Foreign Missions. They would be the first overseas American missionaries. Almost immediately Adoniram was smitten by Ann's vivacity, charm, and beauty, and a month later he formally asked her in a letter if she would consent to have him court her. She replied that he must secure her father's permission.

So it was, in July of 1810, that Adoniram sent her father one of the most extraordinary letters from a prospective son-in-law:

> I have now to ask whether you can consent to part with your daughter early next spring, to see her no more in this world? Whether you can consent to her departure to a heathen land, and her subjection to the hardships and sufferings of a missionary life? Whether you can consent to her exposure to the dangers of the ocean; to the fatal influence of the southern climate of India; to every kind of want and distress; to degradation, insult, persecution, and perhaps a violent death? Can you consent to all this, for the sake of Him who left His heavenly home and died for her and for you; for the sake of perishing, immortal souls; for the sake of Zion and the glory of God? Can you consent to all this, in hope of soon meeting your daughter in the world of glory, with a crown of righteousness brightened by the acclamations of praise which shall resound to her Saviour from the heathens saved, through her means, from eternal woe and despair?[4]

Ann's parents, John and Rebecca Hasseltine, allowed Ann to decide for herself. For her part, Ann was not able to answer Adoniram immediately. First, she barely knew him. And then she realized that to marry Adoniram was to commit herself to a missionary vocation, and she was not initially sure this was what God wanted for her life. As Ann wrote in her diary on September 10, 1810:

> An opportunity has been presented to me, of spending my days among the heathen, in attempting to persuade them to receive the Gospel. Were I convinced of its being a call from God, and that it would be more pleasing to him, for me to spend my life in this way than in any other, I think I should be willing to relinquish every earthly object, and, in full view of dangers and hardships, give myself up to the great work.[5]

For two months she wrestled with her feelings, her love for her family, and her dread of suffering alone in a foreign land. Finally, although many of her friends and acquaintances deemed her decision to leave America a "wild, romantic undertaking,"[6] she came to the conclusion that marriage to Judson and a missionary life was indeed God's will for her life. As she wrote to a friend:

> I have about come to the determination to give up all my comforts and enjoyment here, sacrifice my affection to relatives and friends, and go where God, in his providence, shall see fit to place me. My determinations are not hasty, or formed without viewing the dangers, trials, and hardships attendant on a missionary life. . . . [M]y determinations [were] formed . . . with a sense of my obligations to God, and with a full conviction of its being a call in providence, and consequently my duty.[7]

About twenty months later, on February 5, 1812, Ann and Adoniram were married in the Hasseltine home where they had first met. The very next day was the ordination of Adoniram in Tabernacle Congregationalist Church in Salem along with three other Congregationalist missionaries for service in the Indian subcontinent: Samuel Nott (1788–1869), Gordon Hall (1784–1826), and Samuel Newell (1784–1821), with a fourth, Luther Rice (1783–1836), being added at the last moment. Two thousand crowded into the meetinghouse. A hush pervaded the crowd until the moment of ordination, when a wave of weeping and sighing swept through the congregation.[8] Within two weeks the missionaries had all set sail for India: the Judsons and Samuel Newell and his wife Harriet (1793–1812) from Salem, the others and their wives from Philadelphia.

"We Are Confirmed Baptists"

Ann spent most of her time on the voyage to India in reading. Now, one subject that particularly occupied her and Adoniram was baptism. A few years earlier, from 1808 to 1810, when Adoniram was still at Andover Theological Seminary, Adoniram had begun working on an English translation of the Greek New Testament and, among other grammatical and linguistic issues, had found himself perplexed on how to translate the Greek word *baptizō*. Also in going to India, he anticipated having to meet William Carey, Joshua Marshman (1768–1837), and William Ward (1769–1823), three convinced Baptists who were at Serampore, and having to give a response to any questions they might pose to him about the proper subjects of Christian baptism.[9] The four-month voyage to India from February 19 to June 17, 1812, provided an ideal context in which both he and his wife could intensely study this subject afresh. Ann and Adoniram thought that by studying this subject they would furnish themselves with material to defend paedobaptism. Little did they dream what would happen.

Ann Judson summed up so well what transpired during that significant voyage in 1812 in a letter that she wrote to a friend in America. The day before she wrote the letter, September 6, 1812, she and her husband had been baptized as believers by William Ward in the Lall Bazar Chapel in Calcutta.

> You may, perhaps, think this change very sudden, as I have said nothing of it before; but, my dear girl, this alteration hath not been the work of an hour, a day, or a month. The subject has been maturely, candidly, and, I hope, prayerfully examined for months. An examination of the subject of baptism commenced on board the *Caravan*.[10] As Mr. Judson was continuing the translation of the New Testament, which he began in America, he had many doubts respecting the meaning of the word *baptize*. This, with the idea of meeting the Baptists at Serampore, when he would wish to defend his own sentiments induced a more thorough examination of the foundation of the Pedobaptist system. The more he examined, the more his doubts increased; and, unwilling as he was to admit it, he was afraid the Baptists were right and he wrong. After we arrived

at Calcutta, his attention was turned from this subject to the concerns of the mission, and the difficulties with Government. But as his mind was still uneasy, he again renewed the subject. I felt afraid he would become a Baptist, and frequently urged the unhappy consequences if he should. But he said his duty compelled him to satisfy his own mind, and embrace those sentiments which appeared most concordant with Scripture. I always took the Pedobaptist side in reasoning with him, even after I was as doubtful of the truth of their system as he. We left Serampore to reside in Calcutta a week or two, before the arrival of our brethren;[11] and as we had nothing in particular to occupy our attention, we confined it exclusively to this subject. We procured the best authors on both sides, compared them with the Scriptures, examined and re-examined the sentiments of Baptists and Pedobaptists, and were finally compelled, from a conviction of truth, to embrace those of the former. Thus, my dear Nancy, we are confirmed Baptists, not because we wished to be, but because truth compelled us to be. We have endeavored to count the cost, and be prepared for the many severe trials resulting from this change of sentiment. We anticipate the loss of reputation, and of the affection and esteem of many of our American friends. . . . We feel that we are alone in the world, with no real friend and no one on whom we can depend but God.[12]

On the *Caravan* the Judsons would have primarily had the Scriptures to examine. When they got to India, they were able to consult a variety of Paedobaptist and Credobaptist works over a two-month period.[13] As Ann told her parents the following year in another letter:

After we removed to Calcutta, he [that is, Adoniram] found in the library in our chamber many books on both sides, which he determined to read candidly and prayerfully, and to hold fast, or embrace the truth, however mortifying, however great the sacrifice. I now commenced reading on the subject, with all my prejudices on the Pedobaptist side. We had with us Dr. Worcester's, Dr. Austin's, Peter Edwards's and other Pedobaptist writings. But after closely examining the subject for several weeks, we were constrained to acknowledge that the truth appeared to lie on the Baptists' side.[14]

Here Ann mentions three specific Paedobaptist authors. Samuel Worcester (1770–1821) was a Massachusetts Congregationalist and an ardent advocate of the theology known as the New Divinity. This theological system was promoted by the heirs of Jonathan Edwards and combined a fresh approach to issues such as the sovereignty of God and the freedom of the will with a careful attention to practical Christianity and the nature of revival. In time, this confluence of theological emphases came to provide a firm foundation for cross-cultural missions. Adoniram's own father, Adoniram Judson Sr. (1752–1826), was also an exponent of this theological perspective, having been mentored by Edwards's confidant Joseph Bellamy (1719–1790). Now, Worcester was the author of two works that dealt specifically with paedobaptism: *Two Discourses on the Perpetuity and Provision of God's Gracious Covenant with Abraham and His Seed* (1805) and *Serious and Candid Letters to the Rev. Thomas Baldwin, D.D. on his book entitled "The Baptism of Believers Only, and The Particular Communion of the Baptist Churches, Explained and Vindicated"* (1807).[15] Adoniram Judson quotes from both of these works in his *Christian Baptism* (1813),[16] which originated as a sermon three weeks after his baptism and sums up in a public document the fruit of the Judsons' research into the nature of baptism.[17] Reading Worcester's work would have brought back sweet memories of the man, for it was in Worcester's Tabernacle Church in Salem that Judson and his fellow missionaries were ordained and commissioned for their mission to the Far East.[18]

The second author mentioned by Ann was Samuel Austin (1760–1830), among whose works was *A View of the Economy of the Church of God as it existed primitively under the Abrahamic Dispensation and the Sinai Law* (1807), which Adoniram also refers to in his *Christian Baptism*.[19] Like Worcester, Austin is to be counted among the New Divinity men. He had very close connections with two of the leading theologians of this school of thought: he had studied under Jonathan Edwards the Younger (1745–1801) and later married Jerusha Hopkins, the daughter of one of the leading Edwardseans of the day, Samuel Hopkins (1721–1803).[20] The third author, Peter Edwards, was an Englishman, who had been a Baptist prior to coming to Paedobaptist convictions. He had subsequently written *Candid Reasons for Renouncing the Principles of Anti-Paedobaptism* (1795), a work that went through a number of editions on both sides of the Atlantic.

In the above quotation Ann does not mention any Baptist authors. Her husband's *Christian Baptism* does indicate explicitly that the Judsons found much food for thought in Abraham Booth's (1734–1806) *Paedobaptism Examined* (1784/1787).[21] Peter Edwards's book noted above was written as a direct response to this work by Booth. Other Baptist figures cited by Judson in his sermon include Henry Danvers (c. 1622–1687), whose *A Treatise of Baptism* (1673) is primarily a defense of believer's baptism;[22] John Gill (1697–1771), the doyen of Baptist theologians in the eighteenth century and one who was especially critical of the baptism of infants;[23] and the Seventh-day Baptist Joseph Stennett I (1663–1713), who was one of the most prominent Dissenters of his day.[24]

As Adoniram and then Ann studied all these works and compared what they read with the Scriptures, "truth compelled" them, as Ann puts it, to acknowledge that the better scriptural arguments lay with the Baptists. It is very evident from both of Ann's letters that Adoniram and Ann began this study as firmly entrenched Paedobaptists. It was only with the greatest of reluctance that they were led to differing convictions. In her diary for that summer of 1812, Ann recorded her prayers for the Holy Spirit of God to direct her search. "If ever I sought to know the truth," she wrote, "if ever I looked up to the Father of lights; if ever I gave up myself to the inspired word, I have done so during this investigation."[25]

In the first letter cited above, Ann is also very aware of some of the consequences entailed by their change in sentiments: it will result in the loss of support, financial and even prayerful, of their Congregationalist friends in New England. And it will also mean identification with a body of churches, the Baptists, which were regarded with great disdain by New England Congregationalists. As Adoniram's early Baptist biographer Francis Wayland noted, in the first couple of decades of the nineteenth century, there was "a strong feeling of sectarian antagonism between the Congregationalists and Baptists."[26] The Judsons, however, were determined to follow biblical truth wherever it led and whatever the cost. Adoniram described such determination at the close of *Christian Baptism* as he pled with his hearers (and later readers):

> My brethren, diligently use the means of discovering the truth. Put yourselves in the way of evidence. Indulge free examination. Though the sun shines with perfect clearness, you will never see that light which others enjoy, if you confine yourselves in a cavern, which the beams of the sun cannot penetrate. Be assured, that there is sufficient evidence on this subject, if you seek to discover it. But if your love for truth is not sufficiently strong to make you willing and strive for the discovery of evidence, God will probably leave you to be contented with error. . . . Therefore, to stimulate your minds to candid and energetic research, prize truth above all things.[27]

"Cut Out for the [Burmese] Mission"

So the Judsons were baptized and had to resign from the Congregationalist missionary body that had sent them to India. They informed the American Board of Commissioners for Foreign Missions of their new perspective as soon as they arrived in India. To the board Adoniram wrote a letter that shines with Christian love, as he explained their change in convictions regarding baptism. This change, he said, was the most distressing event ever to have befallen them, since it would prevent them from working hand in hand with men they counted as dear brethren. They sent Luther Rice, who had also been baptized as a believer, back to America to make contact with American Baptists to raise support from them.

Now, the British East India Company, which had a mandate to rule British possessions in the subcontinent, was intensely hostile toward missionaries in India. The only way that the Serampore Trio—Carey, Ward, and Marshman—had been able to stay was by residing in the Danish colony of Serampore. Thus, within ten days of the Judsons' arrival in India, they were ordered by the company to leave the country. In the providence of God they were ultimately led to Burma, reaching Rangoon on July 13, 1813.

Burma lay then between China and India, hemmed in by mountains on both borders. It was an empire governed by a despotic emperor who ruled by fear. Corruption within the government was endemic, and the laws were cruel. Torture and mass executions were routine and kept the population subservient to their rulers. The religion of the Burmese was Buddhism, which Ann rightly described thus:

> The religion of Burmah, then, is, in effect, atheism; and the highest reward of piety, the object of earnest desire and unwearied pursuit, is annihilation. How wretched a system is this; how devoid of adequate motives to virtue; and how vacant of consolation!

Already living there was Felix Carey (1786–1822), William Carey's son, and Felix's family. In the months that followed, Felix was thrilled to have Adoniram and Ann as missionary coworkers. As he wrote to his father a number of months later about the Judsons, "They [both Adoniram and Ann] are just cut out for the [Burmese] Mission." As Felix continued, "Mr. Judson has a splendid grasp of the [Burmese] language and is the very colleague

I wanted."[28] Felix could have mentioned that Ann too was grow-ing in her grasp of the Burmese language. The Burmese language is not an easy language to learn, for its written form has no capi-tals, no word divisions, and no sentence breaks, but the Judsons persevered, as we shall see.

The missionary partnership between the Judsons and Felix Carey and his wife was not to last. In June of 1816, Carey, Marsh-man, and Ward told Thomas Baldwin (1753–1825) and the other members of the mission board of the Triennial Convention that Felix had "gone into the service of his Burman majesty."[29] More bluntly, and more famously, the elder Carey told his close friend John Ryland Jr. (1753–1825) back in England that his son had "shrivelled from a missionary into an ambassador."[30] But Felix Carey was right about Judson and his wife. As the history of the American Baptist mission to Burma unfolded, it became quite obvious that this couple were indeed "cut out" for Burma.

Ann and Adoniram lived in Rangoon for ten years, from 1813 to 1823, dealing with persecution and various hardships. During this time both of them mastered the language, though this feat did not come without much perseverance. Ann noted in her diary for August 15, 1813:

> I have begun to study the language. Find it very hard and dif-ficult, having none of the usual helps in acquiring a language, except a small part of a grammar, and six chapters of St. Mat-thew's Gospel by Mr. [Felix] Carey.

And as her husband noted at greater length in a letter written in 1816:

> For a European or American to acquire a living oriental lan-guage, root and branch, and make it his own, is quite a differ-ent thing from his acquiring a cognate language of the west, or any of the dead languages [i.e. Latin or Ancient Greek], as they are studied in the schools. . . . When we take up a western language, the similarity in the characters, in very many terms,

in many modes of expression, and in the general structure of the sentences, its being in fair print, (a circumstance we hardly think of,) and the assistance of grammars, dictionaries, and instructers, render the work comparatively easy. But [it is quite difficult] when we take up a language spoken by a people on the other side of the earth, whose very thoughts run in channels diverse from ours, and whose modes of expression are consequently all new and uncouth; when we find the letters and words all totally destitute of the least resemblance to any language we had ever met with, and these words not fairly divided, and distinguished, as in western writing, by breaks, and points, and capitals, but run together in one continuous line, a sentence or paragraph seeming to the eye but one long word; when, instead of clear characters on paper, we find only obscure scratches on dried palm leaves strung together, and called a book; when we have no dictionary, and no interpreter to explain a single word, and must get something of the language, before we can avail ourselves of the assistance of a native teacher. . . . It unavoidably takes several years to acquire such a language, in order to converse and write intelligibly on the great truths of the Gospel. Dr. Carey once told me that after he had been some years in Bengal, and thought he was doing very well, in conversing and preaching with the natives, they (as he was afterwards convinced) knew not what he was about. A young Missionary, who expects to pick up the language in a year or two, will probably find that he has not counted the cost. If he should be so fortunate as to obtain a good interpreter, he may be useful by that means. But he will learn, especially if he is in a new place, where the way is not prepared, and no previous ideas communicated, that to qualify himself to communicate divine truth intelligibly, by his voice or pen, is not the work of a year. However, notwithstanding my present great incompetency, I am beginning to translate the New Testament, being extremely anxious to get some parts of Scripture, at least, into an intelligible shape.[31]

By December 1815, Ann was telling her sisters in America that she and Adoniram "feel quite at home, and can converse with ease on common subjects." She felt that she was Adoniram's equal in speaking the language; but when it came to reading and writing she was "far behind" her husband. What they specially found to be a challenge was conversation about the things of God "on account of the want of religious terms in their language."[32] It is noteworthy that Adoniram refrained from preaching until he had a good grasp of the language and had translated some of the Scriptures into Burmese.

In 1817 Ann and Adoniram were able to print—using a printing press that had been sent to them by William Carey—a summary of Christian doctrine by Adoniram and a catechism by Ann. And that May, Adoniram finished translating the Gospel of Matthew and they printed eight hundred copies of it.[33] Adoniram had begun to preach in August of 1818. And within a year, on June 27, 1819, the first Burman convert, a man named Mong Nau, was baptized as a believer.

By this time Ann was also studying Siamese (today known as Thai), which she found to be not as difficult a language as Burmese. By April 1819, she had translated into Siamese her Burmese catechism and her husband's Burmese Gospel of Matthew. This translation by Ann was the first portion of the Scriptures to be translated into Siamese. Later, she helped Adoniram by also translating the books of Daniel and Jonah into Burmese.[34]

Her Last Words Were in Burmese

In late 1821 Ann decided to return to America for a period of time, owing to a severe problem with her liver. It was a difficult decision to leave Burma and also Adoniram, but it was necessary for the recovery of her health. Ann went via England and finally arrived in America on September 25, 1822. Her health was not sufficiently recovered when she decided to make the return trip to Rangoon by way of Calcutta on June 22, 1823. She arrived in Calcutta in mid-October 1823, and was advised not to proceed to Burma, as war seemed imminent between Great Britain and Burma. But Ann was eager to see Adoniram, so in November she sailed for Rangoon, arriving on December 5, 1823. She had been gone two years and four months in total, and the last letter Adoniram had had from her had been thirteen months before her return!

Immediately upon her return Adoniram and Ann moved to the royal capital of Ava. Within a couple of months of their arrival, the First Anglo-Burmese War (1824–1826) broke out. It was to be the first of three wars fought between the British and the Burmese Empire during the course of the nineteenth century. The war, which began primarily over the control of northeastern India, ended in a decisive British victory and was the longest and most expensive war in British Indian history. Fifteen thousand European and Indian soldiers died, together with an unknown number of Burmese military and civilian casualties. Moreover, the war cost the British between five and thirteen million pounds of sterling (roughly 18.5 billion to 48 billion in contemporary US dollars).

Although the Judsons were Americans, all Westerners became suspect, and Adoniram was imprisoned under horrific conditions. Ann literally saved his life by pleading with government officials to let him live, by daily taking food to him in the prison, and by relentlessly pressuring the government authorities throughout the course of the war to free him. No sooner, though, than Adoniram was released in 1826, Ann fell sick, exhausted by this time of stress, persecution, and the burden of managing things without her husband's help. She died on October 24, 1826, her last words being uttered in Burmese, the tongue of the people she had grown to love.[35]

8

The Christian Faith
of Jane Austen

"The Value of That Holy Religion"

In approaching the novels and writings of Jane Austen, it is absolutely vital to remember that she belongs to the "long eighteenth century" that stretched from the Restoration of the monarchy (1660) to the end of the Georgian era (1830).[1] As such, she grew up and lived in a world where the British state and the Anglican Church were regarded as an organic unity. It was really not until the Victorian era that these two spheres began to split apart, and many Victorian novelists—from Charles Dickens (1812–1870) and Anthony Trollope (1815–1882) to George Eliot (1819–1880) and Thomas Hardy (1840–1928)—used the novel to critique Christianity. As Michael Giffin has reminded us, "[Jane] Austen is a devout Anglican who accepts the canonical truths presented in Jewish and Christian scripture, and who assents to the theological truths presented in the *Book of Common Prayer* (1662)."[2] Giffin has thus argued that Austen ought to be read as "an Anglican author who writes Christian stories."[3] Irene Collins, who taught English literature for many years at Liverpool University, heartily concurs. She has noted that the "unprecedented number of biographies of Jane Austen" that have appeared in recent years

> have failed to recognize a central fact about Jane Austen: she was a deeply religious person. Her Christian convictions have either been ignored or mentioned briefly and with apparent reluctance, as though they formed an embarrassing topic likely to make Jane Austen unapproachable to present-day readers.[4]

This does not prevent her from critiquing elements of Georgian Anglicanism though.

One of the more odious figures in her novels, for example, is the Rev. William Collins, a Church of England clergyman somewhat full of his own importance, who appears in *Pride and Prejudice* (1813). Austen was an astute observer of human nature who was also blessed with a sparkling wit, and some of the most humorous scenes in English literature were written by her hand. Consider her depiction of Collins's proposal of marriage to the heroine of the novel, Elizabeth Bennet. Elizabeth regards Rev. Collins as "a conceited, pompous, narrow-minded, silly man,"[5] but has to endure his proposal in the middle of which the Anglican clergyman informs Elizabeth of his three reasons for wanting to marry her, which abundantly reveal the silliness of the man:

> My reasons for marrying are, first, that I think it a right thing for every clergyman in easy circumstances (like myself) to set the example of matrimony in his parish. Secondly, that I am convinced it will add very greatly to my happiness; and thirdly—which perhaps I ought to have mentioned earlier, that it is the particular advice and recommendation of the very noble lady whom I have the honour of calling patroness [a woman by the name of Lady Catherine de Bourgh, who had secured Collins's appointment to his parish]. Twice has she condescended to give me her opinion (unasked too!) on this

subject; . . . she said, "Mr. Collins, you must marry. A clergyman like you must marry.—Chuse properly, chuse a gentle-
woman for *my* sake; and for your *own*, let her be an active,
useful sort of person, not brought up high, but able to make a
small income go a good way. This is my advice."[6]

On the other hand, in *Mansfield Park* (1814) the hero is Edmund Bertram, who is seeking ordination as an Anglican clergyman. In the first scene that deals explicitly with Christianity, he
rebukes one of the other characters in the novel, Mary Crawford,
who is critical of corporate worship that to her mind "can hardly
be serious even on serious subjects."[7] Then toward the end of the
novel, Mary mocks Edmund by telling him that she expected to
hear of him "as a celebrated preacher in some great society of
Methodists, or as a missionary into foreign parts."[8] But Jane does
not share her mocking tones. As Edmund tells Mary Crawford
earlier in the book—and this is Jane's understanding of what is
involved in pastoral ministry—a minister

> has the charge of all that is of the first importance to man-
> kind, individually or collectively considered, temporally and
> eternally . . . [and] has the guardianship of religion and mor-
> als and consequently of the manners which result from their
> influence. . . . The manners I speak of, might rather be called
> conduct, perhaps, the result of good principles; the effect, in
> short, of those doctrines which it is their duty to teach and
> recommend.[9]

In fact, of the twelve clergymen who appear in her novels,
only "three are pilloried"—Mr. Collins noted above, Mr. Elton
in *Emma*, and Dr. Grant in *Mansfield Park*—and presented as
laughable figures because of personal faults. But there is never a
hint that Jane is critical of their vocation or theology per se.[10] It
also bears noting that Jane's father was an Anglican clergyman,
two of her brothers were ordained—one of whom, Henry, was

definitely an evangelical[11]—and eight or so of her other relatives were ministers.[12]

After an overview of her life and her novels, we will turn to look at Jane Austen's Christian faith as expressed plainly in a prayer that she wrote.

Jane's Family Background

Jane Austen (1775–1817) was born on December 16, 1775, at the Anglican rectory in Steventon, Hampshire, which is about 55 miles southeast of London. She was the seventh child and second of two daughters of George Austen (1731–1805), the rector of the twelfth-century Steventon Church of St. Nicholas, and his wife, Cassandra (1739–1827), the youngest daughter of another clergyman, Revd. Thomas Leigh (1696–1764), of Harpsden, Oxfordshire.

George Austen was the only son of William Austen (1701–1737), a surgeon from Tonbridge, Kent. When William Austen died at the age of thirty-six in 1737—his wife was predeceased—the responsibility for George's welfare and education and that of his sisters Philadelphia (1730–1792) and Leonora (1732–1783) fell to their uncle Francis Austen (1698–1791). George eventually went up to St. John's College, Oxford. He was ordained deacon at Oxford in March, 1754, and then priest at Rochester, Kent, in May 1755. Six years later George Austen was appointed to the parish of Steventon, though he did not actually come to the parish until 1764 after his marriage to Cassandra Leigh, whom he had probably met at Oxford.

George and Cassandra Austen had six sons and one other daughter:

- James (1765–1819), who became a curate and was rector of Steventon from his father's death.
- George (1766–1838), who was epileptic, and at six was sent to a home to be cared for privately.

- Edward (1767–1852), who in 1783 became heir to the property of a second cousin by the name of Thomas Knight; Edward took his name, and in due time became the wealthy benefactor of his mother, brothers, and sisters.
- Henry Thomas (1771–1850), an officer in the army, banker, and entrepreneur, and finally clergyman.
- Francis William (Frank) Austen (1774–1865), who became a distinguished admiral.
- Charles John (1779–1852), who also entered the navy and rose to become an admiral.
- Their eldest daughter, Cassandra Elizabeth (1773–1845), who died unmarried, like Jane.

Jane Austen was privately baptized the day after her birth, December 17, 1775. She was formally received into the church on April 5, 1776, at her father's church in Steventon.

Jane's Early Years[13]

The standard picture of Jane Austen's happy childhood derives from her nephew (James) Edward Austen-Leigh (1798–1874), who, with the help of his half-sister Anna Austen (later Lefroy; 1793–1872) and sister Caroline Austen (1805–1880), wrote the first extended memoir of Jane Austen in 1870. A key aspect of Jane's childhood bears mentioning at this point. In *Pride and Prejudice* (1813), the heroine Elizabeth Bennet notes with regard to her upbringing and that of her sisters, "We were always encouraged to read."[14] The same could be said of Jane. Moreover, she and her older sister Cassandra were inseparable. Their mother used to say, "If Cassandra were going to have her head cut off, Jane would insist on sharing her fate."[15] After a lifetime of being close friends, it is not surprising that three days after Jane died, Cassandra wrote to their niece Fanny Knight: "I have lost such a treasure, such a sister, such a friend as never can have been surpassed,—she was the sun of my life."[16] Apart from two brief periods of schooling away from home—at Southampton (1783) and Reading (1785–1786)—Jane was mainly educated by her father and older brothers.

From early 1787 to June 1793 Jane wrote a large number of literary pieces and epistolary novellas, known as her juvenilia. Those she wished to keep she later copied into three blank copybooks given to her by her father, which she named *Volume the First*, *Volume the Second*, and *Volume the Third*. All in all, there are twenty-seven pieces in these copybooks.

Jane Austen began work on "Elinor and Marianne," an early version of *Sense and Sensibility* (1811), in June 1793, which was said to have been read out to the family about 1795. It was possibly at this time that Austen also began her novella, *Lady Susan*, although the copy of the manuscript (now in the Pierpont Morgan Library, New York) is untitled and was written on paper of which two leaves are watermarked 1805.

In August 1796 Jane visited her brother Edward and his wife, Elizabeth, at their first home, a large farmhouse in Kent. It was while there, or immediately after returning home that October, that she began *Pride and Prejudice* under the title "First Impressions." Jane was the same age as her heroine Elizabeth Bennet at the start of composition ("not one and twenty"[17]). This, the first of her novels to be completed, was finished in August 1797, and offered by her father to the publisher Thomas Cadell in November of that year. The publisher declined it without even looking at the manuscript. The title would be changed, however, after the publication of Margaret Holford the Elder's (1757?–1834) novel *First Impressions, or, The Portrait* in 1801. Austen renamed it *Pride and Prejudice*, taking a phrase from Fanny Burney's (1752–1840) *Cecilia* (1782) as her new title.

Jane decided at this point to finish her other novel-in-waiting, the tale of the two sisters Elinor and Marianne. She worked on this at the same time as *Northanger Abbey*, a parody of Gothic fiction, then all the rage, which Jane wrote in 1798–1799. Under the title *Susan* it was sold for ten pounds to a London publisher by the name of Crosby and Co. in 1803. Crosby never published it and held on to the manuscript for six years. Jane inquired about the manuscript in 1809 and eventually had to pay ten pounds in 1816 to get her own manuscript back! It came out posthumously with *Persuasion* in 1817.

In 1800 George Austen suddenly decided to move his family to Bath, while his eldest son, James, took over as his curate in the parish of Steventon. Jane does not appear to have been thrilled by the prospect of leaving the only home she had known for the twenty-five years of her life, though she eventually reconciled herself to moving to Bath, a city she did not particularly like. In December of the following year, when visiting in the area of Steventon, Jane accepted a proposal of marriage from a certain Harris Bigg-Wither, a socially awkward man six years younger than she who stuttered, but whom she did not love. A number of years later she would advise her niece: "Anything is to be preferred or endured rather than marrying without affection."[18] However, Jane thought better of her acceptance overnight, and broke off the engagement the following day. It was the nearest Jane Austen appears to have come to marriage.[19]

A Published Author

Her father died in 1805, and the following year Jane and her mother and sister left Bath. They lived in a number of places till her brother Edward, who had inherited a large estate, found "a roomy, unpretentious house with six bedrooms in the centre of the Hampshire village of Chawton, near the large manor house that he himself owned."[20] The Austen sisters and their mother moved there on July 7, 1809, and it is from this point that Austen's career as a published writer begins. *Sense and Sensibility* was published in 1811 by Thomas Egerton, a friend of Jane's brother Henry. It was published in three volumes and priced at fifteen shillings. It probably had a print run of one thousand or fewer. It was also anonymous, with the simple attribution on the title page "By a

Lady." The first edition sold out and brought Austen "£140 beside the copyright." *Pride and Prejudice* appeared next in January 1813, priced at eighteen shillings. The print run is not known, but it was probably around 1,500 copies. It was a runaway success, but Austen made no money on it beyond the first edition since Egerton held the copyright.

The planning of *Mansfield Park*—her most ambitious novel and the first to be fully written at Chawton—began some time before 1811. According to Cassandra the work was finished soon after June 1813. It was offered to Thomas Egerton possibly in January 1814. It was published May 1814, priced at eighteen shillings, most probably with a print run of 1,250 copies. By November all the copies were sold, and Austen's profit was at least 320 pounds—more than she received in her lifetime for any of her other novels.

Austen's fourth novel, *Emma*, followed in 1816. According to her sister Cassandra, it was written rapidly in fourteen months between January 21, 1814, and March 29, 1815. Austen offered *Emma* in August or September 1815 to the publisher John Murray. *Emma* was duly advertised in December 1815 and published later that month (though dated 1816 on the title page). Murray printed two thousand copies of *Emma*, which proved too many. In her lifetime Austen received only forty-eight pounds and thirteen shillings for *Emma*, which some consider her finest novel.

A first draft of Austen's fifth novel, *Persuasion*, "a reflection on romantic love and marriage," was written between August 8, 1815, and July 18, 1816. After reworking *Persuasion* in August 1816, Jane Austen wrote a preface for *Northanger Abbey*. That autumn, though, she fell ill with a variety of symptoms: nausea, diarrhea, and fatigue. Some scholars believe that she was suffering from Addison's disease, which involves the failure of the adrenal glands at the top of the kidneys. In her biography of Jane, Carol Shields suggests breast cancer.[21]

Austen could barely write that autumn. The following May—

May 24, to be exact—Cassandra took Jane to Winchester to consult with a physician and get better medical help than was available in Chawton. Ultimately, it was all to no avail. On the evening of July 17, Jane was in great pain. Cassandra asked her sister if she wanted anything, to which Jane replied, "Nothing but death," a quotation from *Pilgrim's Progress*, and prayed, "God grant me patience, Pray for me, Oh Pray for me."[22]

She died at 8 College Street, Winchester, at 4:30 a.m. on July 18 in Cassandra's arms. In December of that same year, 1,750 copies of *Persuasion* and *Northanger Abbey* were published together in four volumes by John Murray, prefaced by Henry Austen's "Biographical notice of the author," the first acknowledgment in print of Jane Austen as the author of her six novels.

Jane Austen once compared her novels to "ivory on which I work with so fine a Brush."[23] They all have definite limits in terms of their content: they deal with the miniature world that Austen knew best—the gentry of the English middle class. The lower and upper classes rarely appear.[24] And while the stirring events of her age are sometimes alluded to—such as the American and French Revolutions, the Napoleonic Wars, the Evangelical Revivals of the eighteenth century, and the upheavals of the Industrial Revolution—what takes center stage are the lives of a few families from the middle-class gentry.[25] In the words of Peter Leithart, Jane "gives us a thick description of small events,"[26] and she did this so well that she is rightly regarded as the outstanding novelist of her day.[27]

The Faith of Jane Austen

Jane "displays an Anglican reticence about religious affections"[28] and is very interested in Christianity as a teacher of morals. Given this, it is not surprising that Jane was not an evangelical.[29] In fact, in 1809, Jane was forthright: referring to a novel by Hannah More, she told her sister Cassandra, "I do not like the Evangelicals."[30] By 1814, however, her attitude had changed. As she told her niece

Fanny Knight (1793–1882): "I am by no means convinced that we ought not all to be Evangelicals, & am persuaded that they who are so from reason & feeling, must be happiest & safest."[31] It is noteworthy that her novel *Mansfield Park*, finished not long before this remark to Fanny Knight, reveals a clear "sympathy with Evangelicalism."[32] That sympathy was especially centered upon the belief that Jane and evangelicals had in common: "Christians should be up and doing in the world."[33] For example, *Mansfield Park* tackles a theme dear to the heart of many late eighteenth-century evangelicals, the abolition of the slave trade.[34] Jane could thus write in the fall of 1814 in a letter to a friend, Martha Lloyd (1765–1843), that her hope during the latter stages of the War of 1812 was: "If we are to be ruined, it cannot be helped—but I place my hope of better things on a claim to the protection of heaven, as a religious nation, a nation in spite of much evil improving in religion, which I cannot believe the Americans to possess."[35] Of course, evangelicals had figured prominently in the wave of religious revival that had swept Britain during the previous twenty years or so, a revival that had seen the evangelical victory in the abolition of the slave trade.

An excellent vantage point to see Jane's faith is one of three written prayers that have been attributed to her and that probably date from Jane's life after the death of her father in 1805,[36] though there are doubts about the authenticity of two of them.[37] The third runs as follows and does seem to have been written by Jane:

> Give us grace, Almighty Father, so to pray, as to deserve to be heard, to address thee with our hearts, as with our lips. Thou art every where present, from thee no secret can be hid. May the knowledge of this, teach us to fix our thoughts on thee, with reverence and devotion that we pray not in vain.
>
> Look with mercy on the sins we have this day committed, and in mercy make us feel them deeply, that our repentance may be sincere, & our resolutions steadfast of endeavouring against the commission of such in future. Teach us to un-

derstand the sinfulness of our own hearts, and bring to our knowledge every fault of temper and every evil habit in which we have indulged to the discomfort of our fellow-creatures, and the danger of our own souls. May we now, and on each return of night, consider how the past day has been spent by us, what have been our prevailing thoughts, words, and actions during it, and how far we can acquit ourselves of evil. Have we thought irreverently of Thee, have we disobeyed thy commandments, have we neglected any known duty, or willingly given pain to any human being? Incline us to ask our hearts these questions, Oh! God, and save us from deceiving ourselves by pride or vanity.

Give us a thankful sense of the blessings in which we live, of the many comforts of our lot; that we may not deserve to lose them by discontent or indifference.

Be gracious to our necessities, and guard us, and all we love, from evil this night. May the sick and afflicted, be now, and ever thy care; and heartily do we pray for the safety of all that travel by land or by sea, for the comfort & protection of the orphan and widow and that thy pity may be shewn upon all captives and prisoners.

Above all other blessings Oh! God, for ourselves, and our fellow-creatures, we implore thee to quicken our sense of thy mercy in the redemption of the world, of the value of that holy religion in which we have been brought up, that we may not, by our own neglect, throw away the salvation thou hast given us, nor be Christians only in name. Hear us Almighty God, for his sake who has redeemed us, and taught us thus to pray:

> Our Father which art in Heaven,
> Hallowed be thy name.
> Thy kingdom come,
> Thy will be done in earth, as it is in heaven.
> Give us this day our daily bread.
> And forgive us our debts, as we forgive our debtors.
> And lead us not into temptation, but deliver us from evil:

> For thine is the kingdom, and the power,
>> and the glory, for ever.
>
> Amen.[38]

The language of this prayer is clearly drawn from the *Book of Common Prayer*, with which Jane was so familiar.[39] It is expressed in the first-person plural and is not at all a piece of literary art; it is a simple, unvarnished prayer to God to be prayed by a group of believers in a family context, probably Jane's own family circle.[40] She is deeply concerned in this prayer with hurting others, a common theme in her novels. As Irene Collins notes, Jane's "characters who experience true happiness are those who think about others."[41] Emma Woodhouse thus commented on the character of Mr. Weston in *Emma*: "General benevolence, not general friendship, made a man what he ought to be."[42] In the same novel, it is Mr. Knightley's concern for Emma's father and Miss Bates that stands as Jane's model of true Christian behavior.[43]

The note of heart sincerity also runs throughout the prayer: "Give us grace, Almighty Father, . . . to address thee with our hearts," and she prays for "mercy" that she might "feel" her sins "deeply" and that her "repentance may be sincere." A remark written by Jane in 1814 on the back of one of her brother James's sermons that has recently come to light would indicate that religious sincerity was keenly prized by Jane: "Men may get into a habit of repeating the words of our prayers by rote, perhaps without thoroughly understanding—certainly without thoroughly feeling their full force & meaning."[44] And linked to this desire for sincerity is a longing for self-knowledge, a freedom from self-deception.[45]

It is not really until the end of the prayer, though, that we hear a specifically Christian note and tone, as Jane pleads with God that she might continue to value her salvation and "that holy religion in which [she had] been brought up," a plea that is specifically made "for his sake who has redeemed us." And with a fervor that matches that of any evangelical, Jane asks God to "quicken our sense of thy mercy in the redemption of the world."[46] As Bruce Stovel observes, these sentiments tell us that "Jane Austen had a deep and sincere religious [Christian] faith."[47] And they are sentiments that would have been heartily endorsed by all the women we have looked at in this book.

Notes

Introduction

1. Lisa L. Moore and Joanna Brooks, "Introduction," in *Transatlantic Feminisms in the Age of Revolution*, ed. Lisa L. Moore, Joanna Brooks, and Caroline Wigginton (Oxford, UK: Oxford University Press, 2012), 7.

2. See Jacqueline Broad, "Margaret Fell," in the *Stanford Encyclopedia of Philosophy*, accessed July 31, 2015, http://plato.stanford.edu/entries/margaret-fell/. Fox had already written *The Woman Learning in Silence* (1656), where Fox challenged those who would limit the Spirit of God to "learned men, old books, and [old] authors" and not allow women to speak in church.

3. On Simmonds, see Patricia Crawford, "The Challenges to Patriarchalism: How did the Revolution affect Women?," in *Revolution and Restoration England in the 1650s*, ed. John Morrill (London: Collins & Brown, 1992), 122.

4. Broad, "Margaret Fell."

5. See B. R. White, *The English Baptists of the Seventeenth Century*, vol. 1, *A History of the English Baptists* (Oxfordshire, UK: Baptist Historical Society, 1996), 136.

6. Cited in ibid., 147.

7. Ibid., 148–49.

8. Richard L. Greaves, "The Role of Women in Early English Nonconformity," *Church History* 52 (1983): 301–2.

9. Amanda Porterfield, "Women's Attraction to Puritanism," *Church History* 60 (1991): 205.

10. Greaves, "Role of Women in Early English Nonconformity," 302; Claire Cross, "'He-Goats Before the Flocks': A Note on the Part Played by Women in the Founding of Some Civil War Churches," in *Popular Belief and Practice*, ed. G. J. Cuming and Derek Baker (Cambridge, UK: Cambridge University Press, 1972), 195–98; Anne Laurence, "A Priesthood of She-Believers: Women and Congregations in Mid-Seventeenth-Century England," in *Women in the Church*, ed. W. J. Sheils and Diana Wood

(Oxford, UK: Basil Blackwell for the Ecclesiastical History Society, 1990), 350–51; White, *English Baptists of the Seventeenth Century*, 146.

11. Crawford, "Challenges to Patriarchalism," 123.
12. Roger Gryson, *Le Ministère des femmes dans l'Église ancienne* (Gembloux, France: Editions J. Duculot, S. A., 1972), 25. See also H. Wayne House, "The Ministry of Women in the Apostolic and Postapostolic Periods," *Bibliotheca Sacra* 145 (1988): 387–88.
13. Eric Metaxas, *Seven Men: And the Secret of Their Greatness* (Nashville: Thomas Nelson, 2013).
14. Jamie Janosz, *When Others Shuddered: Eight Women Who Refused to Give Up* (Chicago: Moody, 2014).

Chapter 1: The Witness of Jane Grey, an Evangelical Queen

1. His real name was John Howman; he was born in Feckenham, Worcestershire, and as historian J. Stephan Edwards notes, it was customary at the time for monks to drop their family surname and to use instead only their forename and the name of the town where they had been born— thus "John de (or *of*) Feckenham," in an interview with Justin Taylor, "The Execution of Lady Jane Grey: 460 Years Ago Today," accessed July 27, 2015, http://www.thegospelcoalition.org/blogs/justintaylor/2014/02/12/the-execution-of-lady-jane-grey-460-years-ago-today/.
2. *An Epistle of the Ladye Jane . . . Whereunto is added the communication she had with Master Feckenham . . . Also another epistle which she wrote to her sister, with the words she spake upon the Scaffold before she suffered* (n.p., 1554), [18–19], spelling modernized. This source is not paginated. The text can also be found in *The Harleian Miscellany* (London: Robert Dutton, 1808), 1:369–71, with the original spelling in which Jane wrote it.
3. Faith Cook, *Lady Jane Grey: Nine Day Queen of England* (Durham, UK: Evangelical Press, 2004), 39. Faith Cook's work has been very helpful in studying Jane Grey, as has the brief essay by Paul F. M. Zahl, *Five Women of the English Reformation* (Grand Rapids, MI: Eerdmans, 2001), 56–74. For a recent biography of Katherine Parr along with an edition of some of her writings, see Brandon G. Withrow, *Katherine Parr: A Guided Tour of the Life and Thought of a Reformation Queen* (Phillipsburg, NJ: P&R, 2009).
4. Cook, *Lady Jane Grey*, 43.
5. Zahl, *Five Women*, 59.
6. On Cranmer, see Michael A. G. Haykin, *The Reformers and Puritans as Spiritual Mentors: "Hope Is Kindled,"* The Christian Mentor, vol. 2 (Ontario, Canada: Joshua Press, 2012), 31–48.
7. "Lady Jane Grey—Biography: Jane and the Seymours—till Somerset's fall (1549/1550)," accessed July 27, 2015, http://www.geocities.ws/jane_the_quene/bio3.html.
8. Cook, *Lady Jane Grey*, 94–99.

9. Ibid., 93.
10. Ibid., 109–10.
11. Ibid., 116.
12. Ibid., 126–27.
13. Ibid., 135–41.
14. Cited in Zahl, *Five Women*, 66–67.
15. Roman Catholicism holds to seven sacraments—baptism, confirmation, auricular confession, the eucharist, marriage, holy orders, and last rites—while Protestants have historically held to two—baptism and the Lord's Supper.
16. Mark 14:22.
17. John 10:9; 15:1–10.
18. Rom. 4:17.
19. See 1 Cor. 11:17–34.
20. *Epistle of the Ladye Jane*, [18–23].
21. Zahl, *Five Women*, 68.
22. Ibid., 69.
23. Ibid.
24. *Epistle of the Ladye Jane*, [24].
25. Cook, *Lady Jane Grey*, 187–88.
26. *Epistle of the Ladye Jane*, [25, 27].
27. Cited in Zahl, *Five Women*, 67n3.
28. J. Stephan Edwards, in interview with Justin Taylor, "The Execution of Lady Jane Grey."
29. Cited in Cook, *Lady Jane Grey*, 198.
30. Ibid., 200.

Chapter 2: Richard Baxter's Testimony about Margaret Baxter

1. Most of this chapter first appeared in Michael A. G. Haykin, *The Reformers as Spiritual Mentors: "Hope Is Kindled"* (Ontario, Canada: Joshua Press, 2012), 143–61. Used by permission.
2. J. N. D. Kelly, *Jerome: His Life, Writings, and Controversies* (New York: Harper & Row, 1975), 183, 187.
3. James A. Mohler, *Late Have I Loved You: An Interpretation of Saint Augustine on Human and Divine Relationships* (New York: New City Press, 1991), 71.
4. Edmund Leites, "The Duty to Desire: Love, Friendship, and Sexuality in Some Puritan Theories of Marriage," *Journal of Social History* 15 (1981–1982): 384.
5. Mohler, *Late Have I Loved You*, 68.
6. Cited in Richard Stauffer, *The Humanness of John Calvin*, trans. George H. Shriver (Nashville: Abingdon Press, 1971), 45.
7. J. I. Packer, "Marriage and Family in Puritan Thought," in his *A Quest for Godliness: The Puritan Vision of the Christian Life* (Wheaton, IL: Crossway, 1990), 259–60.

8. Cited in C. H. George and K. George, *The Protestant Mind of the English Reformation 1570–1640* (Princeton, NJ: Princeton University Press, 1961), 268.

9. Cited in Margo Todd, *Christian Humanism and the Puritan Social Order* (Cambridge, UK: Cambridge University Press, 1987), 100. For further discussion, see Daniel Doriani, "The Puritans, Sex, and Pleasure," *Westminster Theological Journal* 53 (1991): 128–29; Leland Ryken, *Worldly Saints: The Puritans As They Really Were* (Grand Rapids, MI: Zondervan, 1986), 41–42.

10. Cited in Leites, "Duty to Desire," 387.

11. Cited in Todd, *Christian Humanism and the Puritan Social Order*, 113.

12. On the significance of the order of reasons given for the institution of marriage, see Packer, *Quest for Godliness*, 261–62. See also Todd, *Christian Humanism and the Puritan Social Order*, 99–100.

13. Packer, *Quest for Godliness*, 262.

14. *A Christian Directory: or, A Sum of Practical Theology, and Cases of Conscience* II.1, in *The Practical Works of the Rev. Richard Baxter* (1846; repr. Morgan, PA: Soli Deo Gloria, 2000), 1:404.

15. J. I. Packer, "A Man for All Ministries," *Reformation and Revival Journal* 1 (Winter 1992): 56.

16. "Richard Baxter's Love-Story and Marriage," in *The Autobiography of Richard Baxter*, abr. J. M. Lloyd Thomas (Totowa, NJ: Rowman & Littlefield, 1974), 274–75.

17. The best introduction to Baxter's life is the *Autobiography of Richard Baxter*. For a recent biographical study, see Geoffrey F. Nuttall, *Richard Baxter* (London: Thomas Nelson & Sons, 1965). For brief biographical sketches, see J. I. Packer, "Great Pastors—V. Richard Baxter (1615–1691)," *Theology* 56 (1953): 174–79; and Packer, "A Man for All Ministries," 53–74.

    The story of the love relationship of Richard and Margaret is told by Baxter himself in his *A Breviate of the Life of Margaret, The Daughter of Francis Charlton, of Apply in Shropshire, Esq., And Wife of Richard Baxter* (London, 1681) and has been reprinted by John T. Wilkinson, *Richard Baxter and Margaret Charlton: A Puritan Love-Story* (London: George Allen & Unwin, 1928). More recently J. I. Packer has produced an abridgement of the *Breviate: A Grief Sanctified: Passing Through Grief to Peace and Joy* (Ann Arbor, MI: Servant Publications, 1997). For a helpful study of Baxter's overall theology of marriage, see Tim Beougher, "The Puritan View of Marriage: The Nature of the Husband/Wife Relationship in Puritan England as Taught and Experienced by a Representative Puritan Pastor, Richard Baxter," *Trinity Journal* 10 (1989): 131–60.

18. Cited in Nuttall, *Richard Baxter*, 6.

19. Cited in N. H. Keeble, *Richard Baxter: Puritan Man of Letters* (Oxford, UK: Clarendon Press, 1982), 11.

20. Packer, *A Grief Sanctified*, 43.
21. Cited in Keeble, *Richard Baxter*, 12.
22. Cited in Nuttall, *Richard Baxter*, 11.
23. Cited in Keeble, *Richard Baxter*, 12.
24. Richard Baxter, *The Reformed Pastor*, ed. William Brown (1862; repr. Edinburgh: Banner of Truth, 1974), 11.
25. *Autobiography of Richard Baxter*, 79. For an excellent study of Baxter's evangelism, see Timothy K. Beougher, "Richard Baxter and Puritan Evangelism," *Journal of the Academy for Evangelism in Theological Education* 7 (1991–1992): 82–94. See also Gary E. Milley, "A Puritan Perspective on Preaching," *Resource* 2 (Jan.–Feb. 1988): 16–17.
26. Cited in Packer, "Richard Baxter," 175.
27. Wilkinson, *Richard Baxter and Margaret Charlton*, 70.
28. Ibid., 78, 81.
29. Ibid., 107.
30. Ibid., 73–74. Also see Packer, *A Grief Sanctified*, 21–22.
31. Wilkinson, *Richard Baxter and Margaret Charlton*, 75–77.
32. Nuttall, *Richard Baxter*, 93.
33. *Autobiography of Richard Baxter*, 173–74; Wilkinson, *Richard Baxter and Margaret Charlton*, 109. But even after his own marriage he could urge ministers to think twice about getting married: Wilkinson, *Richard Baxter and Margaret Charlton*, 155–58; *Christian Directory* II.1, in *Practical Works of the Rev. Richard Baxter*, 1:400–401. See also Beougher, "Puritan View of Marriage," 152.
34. Wilkinson, *Richard Baxter and Margaret Charlton*, 155–56.
35. Ibid., 110.
36. Ibid., 132, 135–36, 142.
37. Ibid., 129.
38. *Christian Directory* II.7, in *Practical Works of the Rev. Richard Baxter*, 1:436.
39. Wilkinson, *Richard Baxter and Margaret Charlton*, 106–7. See also 116–17, 134–35, where Baxter gives other reasons for her fearfulness.
40. Ibid., 146.
41. Ibid., 106.
42. Ibid., 137.
43. Ibid., 132, 135.
44. Ibid., 129.
45. Ibid., 136.
46. Ibid., 111–14.
47. Ibid., 113.
48. Ibid., 129.
49. Ibid., 127.
50. Ibid.
51. Ibid., 126.

52. Bo Salisbury, *Good Mr. Baxter: Sketches of Effective, Caring Leadership for the Church from the Life of Richard Baxter*, chap. 10. "Husband," accessed July 27, 2015, http://www.bosalisbury.com/interests/richard-baxter/good-mr-baxter/10-husband/. For a general admonition of husbands to be submissive at times to their wives, see Eph. 5:21.
53. Wilkinson, *Richard Baxter and Margaret Charlton*, 115–16.
54. Ibid., 115–17.
55. Ibid., 118.
56. Ibid., 132.
57. Ibid., 124.
58. A reference to such texts as Rom. 16:2, 3, 6; Phil. 4:3.
59. Wilkinson, *Richard Baxter and Margaret Charlton*, 124.
60. Ibid., 152.
61. *Christian Directory* II.7, in *Practical Works of the Rev. Richard Baxter*, 1:432.
62. Wilkinson, *Richard Baxter and Margaret Charlton*, 155; see also 128–29.

Chapter 3: Anne Dutton and Her Theological Works
1. "The Epistle Dedicatory" to Jean Taffin, *Of the markes of the children of God*, trans. Anne Prowse (London: Thomas Man, 1590), [*iv–v*].
2. Cited in Vivien Jones, ed., *Women in the Eighteenth Century: Constructions of femininity* (London: Routledge, 1990), 140.
3. Most of Anne's works have survived in only a few copies. Thankfully her works are currently available in an edition being published by Mercer University Press: *Selected Spiritual Writings of Anne Dutton: Eighteenth-Century, British-Baptist, Woman Theologian* (2003–), ed. JoAnn Ford Watson, 6 vols.
4. *A Brief Account of the Gracious Dealings of God, with a Poor, Sinful, Unworthy Creature* (1750), in Watson, *Selected Spiritual Writings of Anne Dutton*, 3:47, 50.
5. For his story, see the excellent little study by B. A. Ramsbottom, *The Puritan Samson: The Life of David Crosley 1669–1744* (Hertfordshire, UK: Gospel Standard Trust, 1991).
6. *God's Operations of Grace: but No Offers of Grace* (London: D. Bridge, 1707), 163, 209.
7. *Brief Account of the Gracious Dealings of God*, in Watson, *Selected Spiritual Writings of Anne Dutton*, 3:51.
8. Ibid., 3:70.
9. Michael D. Sciretti Jr., "'Feed My Lambs': The Spiritual Direction Ministry of Calvinistic British Baptist Anne Dutton During the Early Years of the Evangelical Revival," PhD thesis, Baylor University (2009), 77.
10. Cited in Sciretti, "'Feed My Lambs,'" 91.
11. Ibid., 91–92.

12. For the quotations in this paragraph, see Stephen J. Stein, "A Note on Anne Dutton, Eighteenth-Century Evangelical," *Church History* 44 (December 1975): 488–89.
13. Sciretti, "'Feed My Lambs,'" 100–101.
14. *A letter to such of the Servants of Christ, who may have any scruple about the Lawfulness of Printing any thing written by a Woman*, in Watson, *Selected Spiritual Writings of Anne Dutton*, 3:254.
15. Ibid.
16. Ibid., 3:257.
17. Ibid., 3:256.
18. *Mr. Sanddeman Refuted by An Old Woman* (London: J. Hart, 1761), in *Selected Spiritual Writings of Anne Dutton*, 5:41–75.
19. *A Letter on the Divine Eternal Sonship of Jesus Christ* (London: J. Hart, 1757), in Watson, *Selected Spiritual Writings of Anne Dutton*, 5:1–13.
20. Both of these can be found in Watson, *Selected Spiritual Writings of Anne Dutton*, 1:5–84. For the conflict between Wesley and Dutton, see Arthur Wallington, "Wesley and Anne Dutton," *Proceedings of the Wesley Historical Society* 11 (June 1918): 43–48.
21. For this letter to Whitefield, see also Watson, *Selected Spiritual Writings of Anne Dutton*, 1:1–4.
22. *Letter . . . to the Reverend Mr. George Whitefield*, in Watson, *Selected Spiritual Writings of Anne Dutton*, 1:2.
23. Ibid., 1:2–3.
24. Ibid., 1:3; emphasis original.
25. See Derek R. Moore-Crispin, " 'The Real Absence': Ulrich Zwingli's View of the Lord's Supper," in *Union and Communion, 1529–1979* (London: Westminster Conference, 1979), 22–34.
26. Victor A. Shepherd, *The Nature and Function of Faith in the Theology of John Calvin* (Macon, GA: Mercer University Press, 1983), 220. Other helpful studies on Calvin's theology of the Lord's Supper include B. A. Gerrish, "The Lord's Supper in the Reformed Confessions," *Theology Today* 13 (1966–1967): 224–43; John D. Nicholls, "'Union with Christ': John Calvin on the Lord's Supper," in *Union and Communion*, 35–54; John Yates, "Role of the Holy Spirit in the Lord's Supper," *Churchman* 105 (1991): 355–56; B. A. Gerrish, *Grace and Gratitude: The Eucharistic Theology of John Calvin* (Minneapolis: Fortress Press, 1993).
27. *Thoughts on the Lord's Supper, Relating to the Nature, Subjects, and right Partaking of this Solemn Ordinance* (London: J. Hart, 1748), 3–4.
28. Ibid., 21.
29. Gordon D. Fee, *The First Epistle to the Corinthians* (Grand Rapids, MI: Eerdmans, 1987), 370.
30. *Thoughts on the Lord's Supper*, 25; see also, 56.
31. Ibid., 7

32. Letter to John Robinson, November 30, 1766, in Timothy Whelan, "Six Letters of Robert Robinson from Dr Williams's Library," *The Baptist Quarterly*, 39, no.7 (July 2002): 355–56.

Chapter 4: Sarah Edwards and the Vision of God

1. For Edwards as theologian of revival, see Michael A. G. Haykin, *Jonathan Edwards: The Holy Spirit in Revival* (Durham, UK: Evangelical Press, 2005). The bulk of this chapter is taken from this work and used with permission.
2. *The Great Awakening*, vol. 4, *The Works of Jonathan Edwards*, ed. C. C. Goen (New Haven, CT: Yale University Press, 1972), 65n9.
3. Ibid., 499.
4. Iain H. Murray, *Jonathan Edwards—A New Biography* (Edinburgh: Banner of Truth, 1987), 237–38.
5. Goen, ed., *Great Awakening*, 293–347.
6. Ibid., 348–83. Quote is from page 348.
7. Ibid., 384–408.
8. Ibid., 409–95.
9. Ibid., 496–530.
10. Ibid., 411.
11. Ibid., 331–41. For Sarah's own account that Jonathan drew upon for his rendition, see Sereno E. Dwight, "Memoirs of Jonathan Edwards, A. M," in *The Works of Jonathan Edwards* (Edinburgh: Banner of Truth, 1987), 1:*lxii–lxviii*.
12. Amanda Porterfield, *Feminine Spirituality in America: From Sarah Edwards to Martha Graham* (Philadelphia: Temple University Press, 1980), 49.
13. *Letters and Personal Writings*, ed. George S. Claghorn, vol. 16, *The Works of Jonathan Edwards* (New Haven, CT: Yale University Press, 1998), 789–90. For a study of Sarah's life, see Elisabeth D. Dodds, *Marriage To a Difficult Man. The Uncommon Union of Jonathan & Sarah Edwards* (1971; repr. Laurel, MS: Audubon Press, 2004). For smaller studies, see Ethel Wallace, "A Colonial Parson's Wife: Sarah Pierrepont Edwards 1710–1758: 'And a Very Eminent Christian,'" *The Review and Expositor* 47 (1950): 41–56; Ruth A. Tucker, *First Ladies of the Parish. Historical Portraits of Pastors' Wives* (Grand Rapids, MI: Zondervan, 1988), 73–81; Noël Piper, "Sarah Edwards: Jonathan's Home and Haven," in *A God Entranced Vision of All Things: The Legacy of Jonathan Edwards*, ed. John Piper and Justin Taylor (Wheaton, IL: Crossway, 2004), 55–78.
14. Leonard I. Sweet notes that the word *sweet* was "incontestably Edwards's favorite word." "The Laughter of One: Sweetness and Light in Franklin and Edwards," in *Benjamin Franklin, Jonathan Edwards, and the Representation of American Culture*, ed. Barbara B. Oberg and Harry S. Stout (New York: Oxford University Press, 1993), 126.

15. "A short Sketch of Mrs. Edwards's Life and Character," appendix 1 to his *Memoirs of the Life, Experience and Character of the Late Rev. Jonathan Edwards, A.M.*, in *The Works of President Edwards* (1817; repr. New York: Burt Franklin, 1968), 1:94. See also the remarks of Porterfield, *Feminine Spirituality*, 39–40.

16. The author initially sent this piece to Douglas Sweeney, the *director of the Jonathan Edwards Center at Trinity Evangelical Divinity School*, to confirm its authenticity. He, in turn, sent it to Kenneth Minkema, the executive editor of the *Works of Jonathan Edwards* and of the Jonathan Edwards Center and Online Archive at Yale University, who believes it "may be the real deal" (Kenneth Minkema, email to Doug Sweeney, September 6, 2012).

    The Panoplist and Missionary Magazine United had been founded by the Edwardseans Nathaniel Emmons and Samuel Spring, along with Jedidiah Morse and Jeremiah Evarts, in 1808, men who were in a position to have access to a genuine document like this.

17. "Relic of Mrs. Edwards," *The Panoplist and Missionary Magazine United* 4 (1811–1812): 507. The extracts run onto pp. 508–9.

18. Samuel Hopkins observed that Jonathan "took opportunities to converse" with each of his children "in his study, singly and closely, about their souls' concerns; and to give them warning, exhortation, and direction, as he saw need." Once a week, each Saturday night, Jonathan instructed his children in the Westminster Shorter Catechism, "not merely by taking care that they learned it by heart," Hopkins noted, "but by leading them into an understanding of the doctrines therein taught, by asking them questions on each answer, and explaining it to them." *Memoirs of the Life, Experience and Character of the Late Rev. Jonathan Edwards*, in *Works of President Edwards*, 1:46.

19. Goen, ed., *Great Awakening*, 333.

20. For Buell, see Deborah Gill Hilzinger, *"The Ministry of Samuel Buell,"* MA thesis, Columbia University, 1989; and Douglas Dicarlo, *"The Religious Mind-Set of Samuel Buell, Clergyman of Eighteenth-Century Long Island,"* MA thesis, Long Island University, 1994.

21. Dwight, "Memoirs of Jonathan Edwards," in *Works of Jonathan Edwards*, 1:lxii.

22. Dodds, *Marriage to a Difficult Man*, 99. For some of the various analyses of Sarah's experiences, see James Wm. McClendon Jr., *Ethics: Systematic Theology*, vol. 1 (Nashville, TN: Abingdon Press, 1986), 121–23. Also see the excellent recounting and analysis of Sarah's experiences by George Marsden, *Jonathan Edwards: A Life* (New Haven, CT: Yale University Press, 2003), 240–49.

23. See Piper, "Sarah Edwards," 68–72.

24. Goen, ed., *Great Awakening*, 332. For the passage in Sarah's narrative that Edwards is drawing from, see Dwight, "Memoirs of Jonathan Edwards," in *Works of Jonathan Edwards*, 1:lxv.

25. Goen, ed., *Great Awakening*, 333.
26. Ibid., 336.
27. Ibid., 339.
28. Julie Ellison, "The Sociology of 'Holy Indifference': Sarah Edwards' Narrative," *American Literature* 56 (1984): 489.
29. Goen, ed., *Great Awakening*, 332.
30. Ibid., 336.
31. Ibid., 336.
32. Ibid., 337.
33. Ibid., 332; also 333. Guy Chevreau (*Catch the Fire: The Toronto Blessing: An experience of renewal and revival* [London: HarperCollins, 1994], 83) wrongly maintains that on one of these occasions Sarah so lost bodily strength that "she apparently fell face-first into her supper." Neither Edwards's account in *Some Thoughts* nor Sarah's own narrative affirm any such thing.
34. Goen, ed., 334–35.
35. Ibid., 341.
36. Ibid., 335.
37. Ibid., 253.
38. Ibid., 255.
39. Ibid., 335.
40. Ibid., 339.
41. Ibid., 340.
42. Ibid.
43. Ibid., 341.
44. Porterfield, *Feminine Spirituality*, 44.
45. Goen, ed., *Great Awakening*, 338–39.
46. "Two Dissertations, II. The Nature of True Virtue," in *Ethical Writings*, ed. Paul Ramsey, vol. 8, *The Works of Jonathan Edwards* (New Haven, CT: Yale University Press, 1989), 542. For a recent discussion of this treatise, see Philip L. Quinn, "The Master Argument of *The Nature of True Virtue*," *Jonathan Edwards: Philosophical Theologian*, ed. Paul Helm and Oliver D. Crisp (Burlington, VT: Ashgate, 2003), 79–97.
47. Ramsey, ed., *Ethical Writings*, 543.
48. McClendon, *Ethics*, 125. McClendon's whole discussion of this point has been extremely helpful in understanding this section of Edwards's *Some Thoughts*; see his *Ethics*, 124–26.
49. Samuel Hopkins, "The Life and Character of the Late Reverend Mr. Jonathan Edwards," in *Jonathan Edwards: A Profile*, ed. David Levin (New York: Hill and Wang, 1969), 80.
50. McClendon, *Ethics*, 127. See also Porterfield, *Feminine Spirituality*, 42–43.

Chapter 5: Anne Steele and Her Hymns

1. The quote is from the inscription on Anne Steele's grave. I am indebted to Tracey Richards for this transcription.

   I am deeply indebted for this chapter to Sharon James, "Anne Steele (1717–1778)," unpublished paper, 1999. For other material on Anne Steele, see Karen Smith, "The Community and the Believers: A Study of Calvinistic Baptist Spirituality in Some Towns and Villages of Hampshire and the Borders of Wiltshire, c.1730–1830," DPhil dissertation, Regent's Park College, University of Oxford, 1986; J. R. Broome, *A Bruised Reed: The Life and Times of Anne Steele* (Hertfordshire, UK: Gospel Standard Trust, 2007); Nancy Jiwon Cho, "'The Ministry of Song': Unmarried British Women's Hymn Writing, 1760–1936," PhD thesis, Durham University (2007), 43–84; Cynthia Y. Aalders, *To Express the Ineffable: The Hymns and Spirituality of Anne Steele* (Milton Keynes, UK: Paternoster, 2008); and Priscilla Chan, *Anne Steele and Her Spiritual Vision: Seeing God in the Peaks, Valleys and Plateaus of Life* (Grand Rapids, MI: Reformation Heritage, 2012).

2. Matthew W. Ward, "Book Reviews: *To Express the Ineffable: The Hymns and Spirituality of Anne Steele.* By Cynthia Y. Aalders," *Southwestern Journal of Theology* 53 (Spring 2011): 227.

3. For the early history of the congregation, see Rosalind Johnson, "Early Baptists in Wiltshire and Hampshire: The Evidence of the Porton and Broughton Baptist Church Book, 1655–1689," a paper presented to the Ecclesiastical History Society Postgraduate Colloquium, University of Manchester, February 4, 2011.

4. Robert W. Oliver, "Book Reviews: *A Bruised Reed: The Life and Times of Anne Steele.* J. R. Broome," *Banner of Truth* 535 (April 2008): 26.

5. Edward Compton, *A History of the Baptist Church, Broughton, Hampshire: from the year 1653 to the present time, compiled from the old church books* (Leicester, UK 1878), 15–16.

6. These journals form part of the Steele Collection in the Angus Library, Regent's Park College, University of Oxford.

7. For the information about Broughton Church in this section, I am indebted to the research done by Smith, "The Community and the Believer."

8. Marjorie Reeves, *Pursuing the Muses: Female Education and Nonconformist Culture, 1700–1900* (London: Leicester University Press, 1997). This work includes a discussion of Anne Steele's work and her circle of friends. Marjorie Reeves has done extensive research on the Nonconformists of Hampshire and Wiltshire, much of it based on valuable primary sources from her own family.

9. Reeves, *Pursuing the Muses*, 27–28.

10. John Westmacott, "Anne Steele 1717–1778 Hymn-Writer," *Our Inheritance* (Summer 1999): 8.

11. Oliver, "Book Reviews: *A Bruised Reed*," 26.

12. Ibid.
13. Michael F. Dixon and Hugh F. Steele-Smith, "Anne Steele's Health: A Modern Diagnosis," *Baptist Quarterly* 32 (July 1988): 351–56.
14. Ibid., 354.
15. Ibid., 351 and notes.
16. Anne Steele Papers, STE 1/5 (Angus Library, Regent's Park College, Oxford).
17. See Jiwon Cho, "Ministry of Song," 43–48. I am indebted to Matthew Crawford, during his doctoral studies at Durham University, for access to this thesis.
18. This letter is held in the Angus Library. It is addressed on the outside to "Mrs Steele." Convention dictated that an unmarried woman of superior social status be addressed as "Mrs," whether married or single. Anne Steele, though unmarried, was often referred to as "Mrs Steele."
19. Anne Steele Papers, STE 3/10 iii (Angus Library, Regent's Park College, Oxford).
20. Jiwon Cho, "Ministry of Song," 77–78.
21. *A Collection of Hymns Adapted to Public Worship*, 3rd ed. (Bristol, UK: W. Pine, 1778), hymn 145.
22. On the free offer of the gospel in Steele's hymns, see further Sharon James, *In Trouble and in Joy: Four Women Who Lived for God* (Durham, UK: Evangelical Press, 2003), 154.
23. *Collection of Hymns Adapted to Public Worship*, hymn 388, stanzas 4–6.
24. Ibid., hymn 79, stanzas 1, 5–6.
25. Ibid., hymn 263, stanzas 1–2.

Chapter 6: Esther Edwards Burr on Friendship

1. Diogenes Allen, *Love: Christian Romance, Marriage, Friendship* (Cambridge, MA: Cowley, 1987), 45–46.
2. C. S. Lewis, *The Screwtape Letters*, Letter 10, in *The Best of C. S. Lewis* (Washington, DC: Canon Press, 1969), 43.
3. "Friendship," in *Dictionary of Biblical Imagery*, ed. Leland Ryken et al. (Downers Grove, IL: InterVarsity Press, 1998), 308–9.
4. R. Paul Stevens, "Friendship," in *The Complete Book of Everyday Christianity*, ed. Robert Banks and R. Paul Stevens (Downers Grove, IL: InterVarsity Press, 1997), 439. Also note 1 Sam. 23:16–18, where Jonathan seeks to strengthen his friend David in the Lord, not on the basis of their relationship. For an example of this kind of friendship in the New Testament, see John 11:11, 35–36.
5. In the New Testament, see 2 John 12.
6. For a study of their friendship, see Lucia Bergamasco, "Amitié, amour et spiritualité dans la Nouvelle-Angleterre du XVIIᵉ siècle: l'expérience d'Esther Burr et de Sarah Prince," *Annales ESC* 41 (1986): 295–323. For a study of Sarah Prince, see Lucia Bergamasco, "Female education and spiritual life: the case of ministers' daughters," in *Current Issues in*

Women's History, ed. Arina Angerman et al. (New York: Routledge, 1989), 39–60.

7. Cited in Carol F. Karlsen and Laurie Crumpacker, eds., *The Journal of Esther Edwards Burr 1754–1757* (New Haven, CT: Yale University Press, 1984), 8. For a very brief biographical sketch of Esther, see Gerald R. McDermott, "Burr, Esther Edwards," in *The Blackwell Dictionary of Evangelical Biography 1730–1860*, ed. Donald M. Lewis (Cambridge, MA: Blackwell, 1995), 1:175. See also the helpful chapter, "Through Esther's Eyes," in Iain H. Murray, *Jonathan Edwards—A New Biography* (Edinburgh: Banner of Truth, 1987), 399–420. Also see the various references in George M. Marsden, *Jonathan Edwards: A Life* (New Haven, CT: Yale University Press, 2003), passim.

8. Sereno E. Dwight ("Memoirs of Jonathan Edwards, A. M.," in *The Works of Jonathan Edwards* [1834; repr. Edinburgh: Banner of Truth, 1987], 1:*clxxix*) notes that Esther "appeared to be the subject of divine impressions, when seven or eight years old." Cf., e.g., the impression made upon a six-year-old Bethan Lloyd-Jones, née Phillips, by the Welsh Revival of 1904–1905, in Bethan Lloyd-Jones, "Memories of the 1904–05 revival in Wales," *Evangelicals Now* 20 (January 2005): 15–18.

9. Karlsen and Crumpacker, eds., *Journal of Esther Edwards Burr*, 9.

10. Dwight, "Memoirs," in *Works*, 1:*clxxix*; Karlsen and Crumpacker, eds., *Journal of Esther Edwards Burr*, 12.

11. On Burr, see Randall Blamer, "Burr, Aaron," in *Blackwell Dictionary of Evangelical Biography*, 1:175.

12. Cited in Marsden, *Jonathan Edwards*, 392.

13. Cited in Herbert S. Parmet and Marie B. Hecht, *Aaron Burr: Portrait of an Ambitious Man* (New York: Macmillan, 1967), 1–2. Esther is wrongly called "Sarah" in this book.

14. Karlsen and Crumpacker, eds., *Journal of Esther Edwards Burr*, 13.

15. Entry for February 15, 1755; Karlsen and Crumpacker, eds., *Journal of Esther Edwards Burr*, 92. The spelling and emphases in this entry and subsequent ones are Esther's.

16. Murray, *Jonathan Edwards*, 401.

17. Karlsen and Crumpacker, eds., *Journal of Esther Edwards Burr*, 14–15. See also Murray, *Jonathan Edwards*, 402.

18. Karlsen and Crumpacker, eds., *Journal of Esther Edwards Burr*, 207, 208, and 216.

19. Ibid., 15.

20. Ibid., 224.

21. Ibid., 237, 243.

22. Ibid., 168, 245.

23. Ibid., 243.

24. Ibid., 124.

25. Entry for April 20, 1755, in ibid., 112.

26. Cited in *The Works of Nathanael Emmons, D.D.*, ed. Jacob Ide (Boston: Congregational Board of Publication, 1861), 1:115.
27. Entry for January 23, 1756, in Karlsen and Crumpacker, eds., *Journal of Esther Edwards Burr*, 185.
28. Ibid., 53.
29. Ibid., 118.
30. Ibid., 50.
31. Ibid., 92.
32. Ibid., 185.
33. Ibid., 257. On Ewing, see "Penn Biographies: John Ewing (1732–1802)," accessed July 30, 2015, http://www.archives.upenn.edu/people/1700s/ewing_john.html.
34. See also Marsden, *Jonathan Edwards*, 420.
35. Murray, *Jonathan Edwards*, 9.
36. On Jonathan's sisters, see Kenneth P. Minkema, "Hannah and Her Sisters: Sisterhood, Courtship, and Marriage in the Edwards Family in the Early Eighteenth Century," *New England Historical and Genealogical Register* 146 (January 1992): 35–56.

Chapter 7: Ann Judson and the Missionary Enterprise

1. Cited in Leslie K. Tarr, "Ann Judson—Woman of Courage," *Decision*, Canadian ed., 33 (October 1994): 25.
2. Among the most important of those accounts are the following: Edward Judson, *Adoniram Judson: A biography* (c. 1883; repr. Philadelphia: American Baptist Publication Society, 1894); Courtney Anderson, *To the Golden Shore: The Life of Adoniram Judson* (1956; repr. Valley Forge, PA: Judson Press, 1987); Sharon James, *My Heart in His Hands: Ann Judson of Burma: A Life with Selections from Her Memoir and Letters* (Durham, UK: Evangelical Press, 1998). For Ann's own account of her life, see *An Account of the American Baptist Mission to the Burman Empire in a Series of Letters Addressed to a Gentleman in London* (London: Joseph Butterworth, 1823).
3. Cited in James, *My Heart in His Hands*, 27.
4. Ibid., 33, 35.
5. Ibid., 36.
6. Ann Hassletine, Diary, October 28, 1810, in ibid., 37.
7. Ann Hasseltine, Letter to Lydia Kimball, September 8, 1810, in ibid., 39.
8. Anderson, *To the Golden Shore*, 112.
9. In actuality, the Serampore brethren appear to have made it a matter of principle never to raise this issue with Paedobaptist guests. See Francis Wayland, *A Memoir of the Life and Labors of the Rev. Adoniram Judson, D.D.* (Boston: Phillips, Sampson, 1853), 1:95. See also Carey's account of Judson's thoughts about meeting Carey and his coworkers: Letter to John Williams, October 20, 1812, cited in *Serampore Letters: Being the Unpublished Correspondence of William Carey and Others*

with John Williams 1800–1816, ed. Leighton Williams and Mornay Williams (New York: Putnam's Sons, 1892), 144.

10. The ship on which the Judsons along with their fellow missionaries Samuel and Harriet (1793–1812) Newell sailed to India.

11. A reference to Luther Rice and the other Congregationalist missionaries, Gordon Hall and Samuel and Roxana Nott, who had been commissioned with the Judsons. Luther Rice and the three others arrived on August 10. See William H. Brackney, *Dispensations of Providence: The Journal and Selected Letters of Luther Rice* (Rochester, NY: American Baptist Historical Society, 1984), 68.

12. Ann Judson, letter to a friend, September 7, 1812, cited in Edward Judson, *The Life of Adoniram Judson* (New York: Anson D. F. Randolph, 1883), 38–40.

13. It bears noting that the Judsons did not speak to any of the Serampore Trio about this matter until they had reached a decision to become Baptists. See Adoniram Judson, *Christian Baptism* (Calcutta, 1813), [3]. For the letter, written on August 27, in which they informed Carey, Marshman, and Ward of their desire to be baptized, see *The Story of the Lall Bazar Baptist Church Calcutta*, comp. Edwards Steane Wenger (Calcutta: Edinburgh Press, 1908), 98.

14. Ann Judson, letter to her parents, February 14, 1813, in Judson, *Life of Adoniram Judson*, 40.

15. Both of these works were published in Salem, MA. The *Two Discourses* were revised for a second edition that appeared in 1807 together with the letters to Baldwin. For Worcester's life, see the biography by his son, Samuel Melanchthon Worcester, *The Life and Labors of Rev. Samuel Worcester, D.D.*, 2 vols. (Boston, MA: Crocker & Brewster, 1852). For a brief sketch, see David W. Kling, "Worcester, Samuel," in *The Blackwell Dictionary of Evangelical Biography, 1730–1860*, ed. Donald M. Lewis (Oxford, UK: Blackwell, 1995), 2:1,219.

16. *Christian Baptism*, 6, n.*; 14, n.*; 15, n.†; 33, n.*; 38, n.*; 42, n.*; 57, n.*; 82, n.*

17. This sermon was first preached in Calcutta on September 27. Carey judged it to be "a very excellent discourse" (Letter to John Williams, October 20, 1812, cited in Williams and Williams, eds., *Serampore Letters*, 144), and "the best sermon upon Baptism, that I ever heard" (Letter to William Staughton, October 20, 1812, cited in James D. Knowles, *Memoir of Mrs. Ann H. Judson*, 2nd ed. [London: Wightman & Cramp, 1829], 66).

18. See Anderson, *To the Golden Shore*, 103–14. I have long considered Anderson's life of Adoniram Judson to be the best ever written of the American missionary. I shall never forget the profound impression the book made upon me as I read it one summer during the early 1990s at my brother-in-law's cottage in Port Elgin, Ontario.

19. See Judson, *Christian Baptism*, 62, n.*.

20. For a sketch of Austin's life, see William B. Sprague, *Annals of the American Pulpit: Congregationalists* (New York: Robert Carter & Brothers, 1857), 2:221–28.
21. Adoniram Judson, *Christian Baptism*, [3]. Luther Rice also profited by reading Brackney, *Dispensations of Providence*, 73. See the discussion of this book by Sharon James, "Abraham Booth's Defence of Believer's Baptism by Immersion: A Summary," in *"The First Counsellor of Our Denomination": Studies on the Life and Ministry of Abraham Booth (1734–1806)*, ed. Michael A. G. Haykin and Victoria J. Haykin (Springfield, MO: Particular Baptist Press, 2011), 132–62. Abraham Booth was described by Andrew Fuller, one who knew him well, as "the first counsellor of our denomination," that is, the English Baptists. Cited in Ernest Payne, "Abraham Booth, 1734–1806," *Baptist Quarterly* 26 (1975–1976): 28.
22. Judson, *Christian Baptism*, 76–77, n.‡, where reference is made to *A Treatise of Baptism*. For two studies of Danvers's life and career, see G. Eric Lane, *Henry Danvers: Contender for Religious Liberty* (n.p.: Fauconberg Press, 1972); and Richard L. Greaves, *Saints and Rebels: Seven Nonconformists in Stuart England* (Macon, GA: Mercer University Press, 1985), 157–77.
23. Judson, *Christian Baptism*, 70, n.*; 76–77, n.‡. The standard biographical sketch of Gill is John Rippon, *A Brief Memoir of the Life and Writings of the Late Rev. John Gill, D.D.* (repr. Harrisonburg, VA: Gano, 1992). For more recent studies of Gill and his theology, see George M. Ella, *John Gill and the Cause of God and Truth* (Eggleston, CO: Go Publications, 1995); Michael A. G. Haykin, ed., *The Life and Thought of John Gill (1697–1771): A Tercentennial Appreciation* (Leiden, NL: E. J. Brill, 1997); and Timothy George, "John Gill," in *Theologians of the Baptist Tradition*, rev. ed., ed. Timothy George and David S. Dockery (Nashville: Broadman, 2001), 11–33.
24. *Christian Baptism*, 77, n. ‖ and 79, n.*, both of which cite Stennett's *An Answer to Mr. David Russen's Entitul'd Fundamentals without a Foundation, or a True Picture of the Anabaptists* (London, 1704). For the life and ministry of Stennett, see esp. "Some Account of the Life Of the Reverend and Learned Mr. Joseph Stennett," in *The Works Of the late Reverend and Learned Mr. Joseph Stennett* (London, 1732), 1:3–36; R. L. Greaves, "Stennett, Joseph (1663–1713)," in *Biographical Dictionary of British Radicals in the Seventeenth Century*, ed. R. L. Greaves and Robert Zaller (Sussex, UK: Harvester Press, 1984), 3:205–6; Allen Harrington and Martha Stennett Harrington, "The Stennetts of England," accessed July 30, 2015, http://www.blue-hare.com/stennett/tpgindex .htm#prefixa.
25. Cited in James, *My Heart in His Hands*, 55.
26. Wayland, *Life and Labors of the Rev. Adoniram Judson*, 1:86. See also Adoniram Judson's statement in this regard that he would now be re-

garded by his Congregationalist friends as "a weak, despicable Baptist." Wayland, *Life and Labors of the Rev. Adoniram Judson*, 1:102.

27. Judson, *Christian Baptism*, 88.
28. Cited in S. Pearce Carey, *William Carey*, 8th ed. (London: Carey Press, 1934), 320.
29. William Carey, Joshua Marshman, and William Ward, Letter to U.S. Baptist Board of Missions, June 25, 1816, in "English Baptist Mission," *American Baptist Magazine and Missionary Intelligencer* 1 (1817–1818): 186.
30. Cited in Sunil Kumar Chatterjee, *Felix Carey (A Tiger Tamed)* (Hooghly, West Bengal: Sunil Kumar Chatterjee, 1991), 114. For the remarkable problems surrounding Felix being the Burmese ambassador, see D. G. E. Hall, "Felix Carey," *Journal of Religion* 12 (October 1932): 484–91.
31. In Ann H. Judson, *An Account of the American Baptist Mission to the Burman Empire*, 2nd ed. (London: Joseph Butterworth, 1827), 43–45.
32. James, *My Heart in His Hands*, 82.
33. Judson's first draft of the entire Burmese Bible was not completed until January 1834. Judson, though, was not entirely happy with this first draft, and he immediately began to revise it. It was not until 1840 that he was satisfied, and the entire Burmese Bible was published in a quarto edition, something he regarded as his major literary accomplishment. Francis Wayland noted that Judson deserves to be placed alongside John Wycliffe (c. 1330–1384) and Martin Luther (1483–1546) for the solidity and excellence of his translation work.
34. Dana L. Robert, "Judson, Ann ('Nancy') (Hasseltine)," in *Biographical Dictionary of Christian Missions*, ed. Gerald H. Anderson (New York: Macmillan, 1998), 346.
35. Robert, "Judson, Ann ('Nancy')(Hasseltine)," 346.

Chapter 8: The Christian Faith of Jane Austen

1. Michael Giffin, "Jane Austen and Religion: Salvation and Society in Georgian England," *Persuasions On-Line* 23 (Winter 2002), accessed July 30, 2015, http://www.jasna.org/persuasions/on-line/vol23no1/giffin .html. Also see Gary Kelly, "Religion and politics," in *The Cambridge Companion to Jane Austen*, ed. Edward Copeland and Juliet McMaster (Cambridge, UK: Cambridge University Press, 1997), 149.
2. Giffin, *Jane Austen and Religion: Salvation and Society in Georgian England* (New York: Palgrave Macmillan, 2002), 5.
3. Ibid., 27.
4. Irene Collins, *Jane Austen: The Parson's Daughter* (1998; repr. New York: Hambledon Continuum, 2007), *xi*.
5. Jane Austen, *Pride and Prejudice* (New York: Alfred A. Knopf, 1991), 128 (chap. 24).
6. Ibid., 100–101 (chap. 19).

7. Jane Austen, *Mansfield Park* (New York: Alfred A. Knopf, 1992), 89 (vol. 1, chap. 9).
8. Ibid., 472 (vol. 3, chap. 16).
9. Ibid., 94–95, 96 (vol. 1, chap. 9).
10. Collins, *Jane Austen*, 46–47.
11. Peter Leithart, *Miniatures and Morals: The Christian Novels of Jane Austen* (Moscow, ID: Canon Press, 2004), 15.
12. Collins, *Jane Austen*, 46.
13. For the following sketch of Jane Austen's life, I have drawn heavily from Marilyn Butler, *Jane Austen* (Oxford, UK: Oxford University Press, 2007). This is the same as Marilyn Butler, "Austen, Jane (1775–1817)," *Oxford Dictionary of National Biography* (Oxford University Press, 2004); online ed., accessed October 8, 2013, http://www.oxforddnb.com .libaccess.lib.mcmaster.ca/view/article/904.
14. Austen, *Pride and Prejudice*, 156 (chap. 29). See also Fiona Stafford, *Brief Lives: Jane Austen* (London: Hesperus Press, 2008), 49.
15. Cited in James Edward Austen-Leigh, *A Memoir of Jane Austen*, 4th ed. (London: Richard Bentley & Son, 1879), 15.
16. Cited in William Austen-Leigh and Richard Arthur Austen-Leigh, *Jane Austen: A Family Record*, rev. Deirdre Le Faye (New York: Konecky & Konecky, 1989), 240.
17. Austen, *Pride and Prejudice*, 157 (chap. 29).
18. Letter to Fanny Knight, November 18–20, 1814. *Jane Austen's Letters*, 4th ed., ed. Deirdre Le Faye (Oxford, UK: Oxford University Press, 2011), 292.
19. See Stafford, *Brief Lives: Jane Austen*, 56–57.
20. Butler, *Jane Austen*, 53.
21. Carol Shields, *Jane Austen* (New York: Penguin, 2001), 173–74.
22. Cited in David Nokes, *Jane Austen: A Life* (Berkeley, CA: University of California Press, 1997), 518.
23. Letter to Edward Knight, December 16–17, 1816. Le Faye, *Jane Austen's Letters*, 337.
24. Leithart, *Miniatures and Morals*, 16–17.
25. Ibid., 14.
26. Ibid., 30.
27. Collins, *Jane Austen*, 236.
28. Leithart, *Miniatures and Morals*, 31; Collins, *Jane Austen*, 236: "Religion was to her [that is, Jane] a private matter: to discuss it in a novel would have been a breach of good taste."
29. See the discussion by John Wiltshire, *The Hidden Jane Austen* (Cambridge, UK: Cambridge University Press, 2014), 82–84.
30. Letter to Cassandra, January 24, 1809. Le Faye, *Jane Austen's Letters*, 177. On the influence of Hannah More at this period of time, see Irene Collins, *Jane Austen and the Clergy* (New York: Hambledon & London, 1994), 145–47. See also Collins, *Jane Austen*, 216–17 on Jane's dislike

of evangelical preaching. For other areas where Jane disagreed with evangelicalism, see Collins, *Jane Austen and the Clergy*, 186–88.

31. Letter to Fanny Knight, November 18–20, 1814, in Le Faye, *Jane Austen's Letters*, 292).
32. Kelly, "Religion and politics," in Copeland and McMaster, eds., *Cambridge Companion to Jane Austen*, 156.
33. Collins, *Jane Austen and the Clergy*, 185.
34. Ibid.
35. Letter to Martha Lloyd, September 2, 1814, in Le Faye, *Jane Austen's Letters*, 285.
36. Austen-Leigh and Austen-Leigh, *Jane Austen*, 274n57.
37. Wiltshire, *Hidden Jane Austen*, 78–79. For the textual history of the prayers, see Jane Austen, *Catharine and Other Writings*, ed. Margaret Anne Doody and Douglas Murray (Oxford, UK: Oxford University Press, 1993), 283–84; Bruce Stovel, "'A Nation Improving in Religion': Jane Austen's Prayers and Their Place in Her Life and Art," *Persuasions: A Publication of the Jane Austen Society of North America*, 16 (1994): 185–186.
38. Found in Jane Austen, *Catharine and Other Writings*, ed. Doody and Murray, 247–48. See also *The Prayers of Jane Austen* (Eugene, OR: Harvest, 2015).
39. Collins, *Jane Austen and the Clergy*, 194; Wiltshire, *Hidden Jane Austen*, 79.
40. Stovel, "A Nation Improving in Religion," 185–196, passim.
41. Collins, *Jane Austen*, 50. See also Wiltshire, *Hidden Jane Austen*, 79.
42. Jane Austen, *Emma*, ed. Fiona Stafford (1816; repr. London: Penguin, 1996), 264 (vol. 3, chap. 2).
43. Collins, *Jane Austen*, 50–51.
44. Sam Marsden, "New Jane Austen manuscript criticises 'men repeating prayers by rote,'" *The Telegraph* (February 3, 2014), accessed July 31, 2015, http://www.telegraph.co.uk/culture/books/booknews/10615541/New-Jane-Austen-manuscript-criticises-men-repeating-prayers-by-rote.htm.
45. Stovel, "A Nation Improving in Religion," 193.
46. Collins, *Jane Austen and the Clergy*, 194.
47. Stovel, "A Nation Improving in Religion," 189.

General Index

Aalders, Cynthia Y., 141n1

Account of the American Baptist Mission to the Burman Empire in a Series of Letters Addressed to a Gentleman in London, An (Ann Judson), 144n2

Act of Toleration (1689), 82

Act of Uniformity (1662), 44

Adams, Thomas, 39

American Board of Commissioners for Foreign Missions, 104, 111

American Revolution, 125

Anderson, Courtney, 144n2, 145n18

Anglicans, 57, 117; and the Evangelical Revival, 57–58

Answer to Mr. David Russen's Entitul'd Fundamentals without a Foundation, or a True Picture of the Anabaptists (Stennett), 146n24

Aristotle, 94

Ash, John, 81–82, 86, 88

Augustine, 37–38; on marriage 38, 39

Austen, Anna (later Lefroy), 121

Austen, Caroline, 121

Austen, Cassandra (née Leigh), 120, 123

Austen, Cassandra Elizabeth, 121, 123, 124–25; singleness of, 121

Austen, Charles John, 121

Austen, Edward, 121, 123; taking of the last name Knight by, 121

Austen, Francis, 120

Austen, Francis William (Frank), 121

Austen, George, Jr., 120

Austen, George, Sr., 120, 123; death of, 123

Austen, Henry, 119–20

Austen, Henry Thomas, 121

Austen, James, 120, 123

Austen, Jane, 20, 117–20; baptism of, 121; and the clergymen in her novels, 118–19; copybooks of (*Volume the First, Volume the Second,* and *Volume the Third*), 122; death of, 125; early years of, 121–23; education of, 121–22; faith of, 125–29; family of, 120–21; first extended memoir of (1870), 121; poor health of, 124–25; reception of in the Anglican Church, 121; singleness of, 123; three prayers attributed to her, 126–29; writing career of, 122–25

Austen, Leonora, 120

Austen, Philadelphia, 120

Austen, William, 120

Austen-Leigh, Edward, 121

Austin, Samuel, 109–10

Baldwin, Thomas, 113

Baptists. *See* Baptists, in America; Calvinistic Baptists

Baptists, in America: and the modern missionary movement, 103; New England Congregationalists' disdain for, 111; and the Triennial Convention, 103

Baxter, Margaret (née Charlton), 20, 40, 42–44; conversion of, 43; healing of from consumption, 43–44; marriage of, 45–52; personality of, 46–47

Baxter, Richard, 40, 40–42; chronic ill health of, 41; conversion of, 41; counsel of to ministers on getting married, 45, 135n33; education of, 41; imprisonment of, 48; marriage

Scripture Index